Creative Embroidery
Mixing the Old with the New CHRISTEN BROWN

STITCH & EMBELLISH YOUR STASHED TREASURES

C&T PUBLISHING
Another Maker Inspired!

A Note from the Author

The projects in this book are designed in a way that the reader can use their stash to create a similar piece. Sprinkled throughout the chapters you will also find pieces titled Stash Idea Inspiration, to help inspire you to use your stash of treasures. Enjoy.

Heart Ornament or Pin (page 117)

Scrap Pins (page 133)

DEDICATION

Happy Creating I dedicate this book to you, the reader. I hope that you will always find time to enjoy the creative adventure.

~Christen

UPcyCleD Jell-O Mold (page 138)

SPECIAL ACKNOWLEDGEMENTS

Special thank you to Diane Herbort, co-author of *Old Glories: Magical Makeovers for Vintage Textiles, Trim, and Photos*, for contributing her knowledge of vintage lace, and other invaluable tips. Thanks also to Lynn Woll of Create Whimsy for guiding me through her special finishing technique (see soft-edge assembly on page 107).

Lastly, a big shout out to my book family, Liz, Roxane, Karla, Amy, Gailen, April, Lauren, Tim, and Jennifer, thank you for all that you do!

Stash Contributors

The precious bits of lace, fabric, trims, buttons, and embellishments that grace these pages came from my mom and my grandmother, as well as Richard and Alice, Virginia and Meg, Doug and Diane, Shari and George, Phred and Tom, Betty and Bud, Sylvia, Cynthia, Donna, Sue, Christine, Katrina, Jeri, Aunt Murt, and Auntie B. Thank you, I am truly grateful.

My Biggest Fans

To my husband, Kevin, and daughter, Gwen—thank you for your unconditional love and support and for allowing me to play in my room. Love you both to the moon and back!

Contents

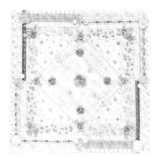

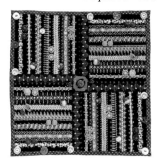

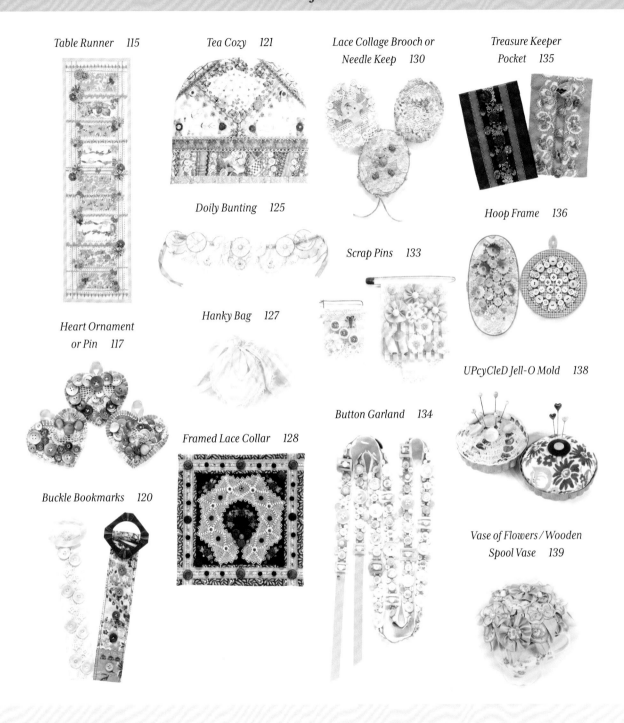

The Visual Guide is meant to be a quick page reference guide. The stitches are arranged in the way that you may use them, or by the threads, ribbons, or embellishments that you would use to stitch them.

INDIVIDUAL AND GROUPED STITCHES

These stitches can be worked as a single unit, onto a border row stitch, or into a vignette. Use cotton or silk floss, silk perle or perle cotton threads, or silk embroidery ribbons.

Cross stitch
(page 72)

Cross stitch twisted
(page 72)

Fleet stitch
(page 73)

Fleet stitch with
loose knot stitch
(page 73)

Fly stitch
(page 73)

Fly stitch offset
(page 73)

Fly stitch with
French knot stitch
(page 73)

Fly with lazy daisy
stitch (page 73)

French knot stitch
(page 71)

Lazy daisy stitch
(page 72)

Lazy daisy with
bullion tip stitch
(page 72)

Lazy daisy with
French knot stitch
(page 72)

Looped tendril
stitch (page 72)

Pistil stitch
(page 71)

Seed stitch
(page 71)

Shell stitch
(page 76)

Stamen stitch
(page 71)

Straight stitch
(page 71)

CONTINUOUS STITCHES

These stitches can be worked along a line, seam, hanky edge, section of lace, or edge of ribbon to create a border row. Use cotton or silk floss, silk perle or perle cotton threads, or silk embroidery ribbons.

Backstitch
(page 74)

Bead strand stitch single
(page 74)

Blanket and chain
stitches (page 76)

Blanket stitch
(page 76)

Blanket stitch closed
(page 76)

Blanket stitch up and
down (page 76)

Chain stitch
(page 75)

Chain stitch double
(page 75)

Chain stitch spiny
(page 75)

Chain stitch zigzag
(page 75)

Chevron stitch
(page 79)

Coral stitch
(page 74)

Couched stitch
(page 74)

Cretan stitch
(page 78)

Cretan stitch looped
(page 78)

Cretan stitch up and
down (page 78)

Cretan stitch with chain
stitch (page 78)

Cretan stitch with feather
stitch (page 78)

Crossed wing stitch
(page 79)

Cross stitch row
(page 79)

Feather stitch
(page 77)

Feather stitch
cobwebbed (page 77)

Feather stitch double
(page 77)

Feather stitch looped
(page 77)

Feather stitch single
(page 77)

Fern stitch modern
(page 77)

Fishhook stitch
(page 75)

Fly stitch fancy link
(page 75)

Herringbone stitch
(page 79)

Herringbone stitch
twisted (page 79)

Shell stitch row
(page 76)

Snail trail stitch
(page 74)

Stem stitch
(page 74)

FLOWER AND SHAPE STITCHES

These stitches can be worked into a vignette, or into a section of fabric. Use cotton or silk floss, or silk perle or perle cotton threads.

Bell flower stitch
(page 81)

Buttonhole circle stitch
(page 81)

Fly stitch flowers
(page 80)

French knot stitch flowers
(page 80)

Lazy daisy stitch
flowers (page 80)

Spiderwebs: corner and round
(page 88)

Spiderweb rose
stitch (page 81)

Spiderweb rose stitch variation
(page 81)

Straight stitch flowers
(page 80)

Whip-stitch rose
(page 81)

Whip-stitch rose variation
(page 81)

Whip-stitch star
(page 71)

SILK RIBBON EMBROIDERY AND RIBBONWORK STITCHES

These stitches can be worked into a vignette or into a section of fabric. Use silk embroidery ribbons; in some cases, additional perle cotton threads are used.

Ellen Matilda's rose stitch
(page 83)

English rose stitch
(page 83)

French knot bud stitch
(page 83)

Heartful stitch
(page 82)

Old rose stitch
(page 84)

Padded straight stitch
(page 82)

Pointed petal stitch
(page 82)

Ribbon loop stitch
(page 83)

Posy stitch
(page 84)

Ribbon stitch
(page 83)

Rosette stitch
(page 84)

Ruched rose stitch
(page 82)

Silk ribbon flower stitch
(page 83)

Woven rose stitch
(page 82)

Woven rose stitch
variation (page 82)

EMBELLISHMENT STITCHES

These stitches can be worked into a vignette, or into a section of fabric. These use a variety of materials such as embroidery threads, silk embroidery ribbons, beads, buttons, sequins, and notions.

Bead cascade stitch
(page 85)

Bead combination stitch
(page 85)

Button bug
(page 88)

Button cascade
(page 87)

Buttonhole decoration
stitches (page 86)

BzzyBee stitch
(page 86)

Clustered buttons
(page 87)

Continuous bead stitch
(page 85)

Curved wing butterfly
stitch (page 86)

Embroidered buttons
(page 87)

Grouped bead stitch
(page 85)

Sequin decoration
stitches (page 86)

Sideview butterfly stitch
(page 86)

Single bead stitch
(page 85)

Snail stitch
(page 86)

Spider stitches (page 88)

Stacked bead stitch
(page 85)

Stacked buttons
(page 87)

Steampunk bugs
(page 88)

Stitched 2-hole buttons (page 87)

Stitched 4-hole buttons (page 87)

A Note from the Author

It is my hope that the projects and gallery pieces included in this book encourage you to use the treasures in your stash. May your creativity flow, and your needles FLY!

Stash Idea Inspiration

This garland was made with 6″ and 7″ (15.2cm and 17.8cm) heart shapes, cut from a vintage cutter quilt. See Heart Ornament or Pin (page 117) for ideas to make a heart-shaped base.

Size: 8″ × 72″ (20.3cm × 1.9m)

Create, Sew, Stitch, and Play Garland

An Enduring Legacy

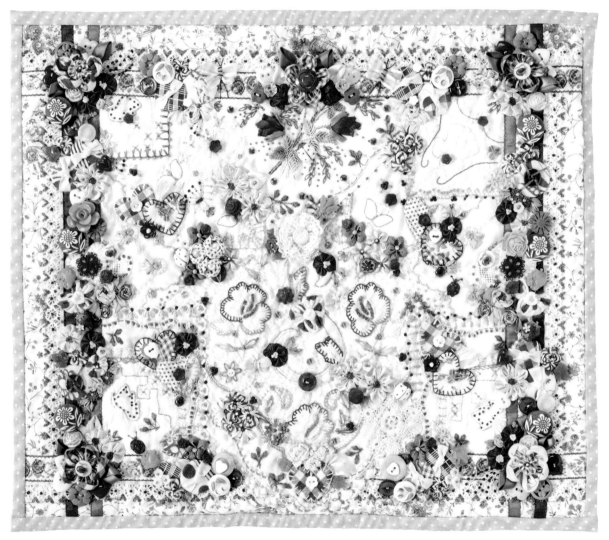

Red Roses, Four Generations of Love, 18¾″ × 16¼″ (47.6 × 41.3cm)

This wallhanging started with several handkerchiefs that belonged to my mother and grandmother. The hankies are collage-pieced together with small bits of fabric, ribbons, laces, and trims. Special mementos include a few tatted and crochet flowers that my mom made, along with glass ladybugs, which is the symbol for our daughter. See Tea Cozy (page 121) and Altering the Past (page 47) for ideas.

EARLY BEGINNINGS

My stash began and was kept in my first sewing box, a gift from my mom on my seventh birthday. It was filled with skeins of floss, packages of needles, bits of felt, sequins, beads, and a variety of trims. I later inherited a needle keep that belonged to my grandmother and a few items from her sewing kit, including the tape measure that I used to create the bracelet Measured Up (below).

The trims came from a promotional offer that was listed on the inside wrapper of seam binding and other trim products made by Wright's manufacturing. My mom sent in her money and a few weeks later a bag full of lace and ribbons arrived. I learned how to sew a rosette from the instructions offered in that package.

My first job was working for Woof and Warp Fabrics, a small chain store in Southern California that specialized in cotton, silk, batik, velvet, and designer fabrics. One of the job requirements was that we made the clothes that we wore to work; as an incentive, we were given a great discount. I of course still have fabric from that job.

I attended the Fashion Institute of Design and Merchandising, intending to build a career in that industry with my love of fabric and design. I quickly learned that my skills were more suited to costuming and one-of-a-kind art creations.

My early stash

Grandmother's felt needle keep

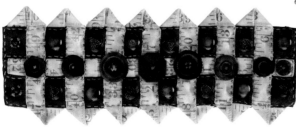

Measured Up, bracelet made from my grandmother's tape measure

WEARABLE ART GALLERY

Pearl's Delight

This jacket began with a box filled with bits of vintage lace and mother-of-pearl buttons given to me by my friend Jeri. The bits of lace are embellished with freshwater pearls and beads, in addition to glass pearls that came from an old necklace that belonged to my grandmother.

Autumn Leaves Must Fall

This short-sleeved jacket began with several embroidered sections that were given to me by another dear friend, Betty. These are combined with a collection of buttons that had been given to me which included Bakelite and celluloid treasures.

Pearl's Delight

Autumn Leaves Must Fall

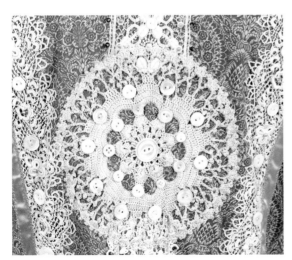

Detail of lace section

Detail of buttons down the back section

Chinoiserie

This vest is made from sections of an embroidered piano shawl, vintage reproduction bark cloth, and silk fabrics. The peach-colored rosettes were made from a gifted length of vintage ombré ribbon. The embroidered sections with metallic threads, silk ribbon embroidery, and embellishments include vintage hand-blown glass beads, abalone shell chips, and carved jade and carnelian charms.

Madame Butterfly

This jacket began with three vintage embroidered sections from China; additional fabrics include solid and silk ikat fabric, cotton, and chintz fabrics. The ribbonwork flowers are made from sari borders, and two-tone ribbons are made by stitching two widths of ribbon together.

Chinoiserie

Madame Butterfly

Detail of piano shawl

Detail of ribbonwork section

What is in Your Stash?

Photo by Felix Mayorca

Your stash probably includes a myriad of treasures that you have acquired through exploring your craft and creating your art. These items may have been passed down through one or several generations of your family, given to you by friends and acquaintances, or purchased at your favorite store.

STAPLE STASH CUPBOARD

To complete the projects in this book, have these essentials on hand in your cupboard. In the following pages, we will explore the vintage items that you can also use.

Materials

- Fabrics: cotton, linen, silk

- Laces and appliqués

- Ribbons and trims

- Embroidery threads: cotton floss and perle cotton

- Silk embroidery ribbons: 2mm, 4mm, and 7mm

- Embellishments: buttons, beads, charms, and sequins

Stabilizers

- Base fabric: bleached cotton muslin

- Fusible interfacing: Pellon 911FF Fusible

- Featherweight interfacing: Pellon SF101 Shape-Flex

- Stabilizers: fast2fuse Double-Sided Heavyweight Fusible (C&T Publishing), Pellon 809 Décor-Bond

- Crinoline fabric: An open-weave, stiffened fabric used for millinery and petticoats

- Batting: Lightweight cotton batting

- Stuffing: Poly-fil (Fairfield Processing Co.)

- Synthetic or wool felt

Did You Know?

Vintage Packaging Labels

Manufacturers used logos and brand names to attract consumers and help them identify with their products. Tips on how to use the products were often included on the packaging label.

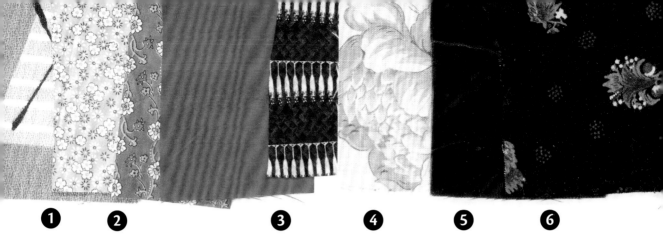

1   **2**   **3**   **4**   **5**   **6**

FABRIC

You can use vintage fabrics for the base of a project or combine them with newer fabrics to create a base.

1. Barkcloth, a woven cotton fabric, has a slightly nubby texture to the touch.

2. Cotton solid and printed fabrics come in a variety of colors and styles.

3. Silk fabrics are available in solid colors and printed patterns in a wide variety of weaves and textures.

Note: *Silk ties and kimonos can be taken apart and used for a base.*

4. Upholstery fabrics made from linen and cotton materials come in solid and printed patterns.

5–6. Velvet has a lush woven pile and was originally made from silk; cotton-velveteen has a lower pile and can be found in both solid and printed colors.

Note: *Discarded flannel or wool garments can also be re-purposed.*

Did You Know?

Woven Cloth

Kimono, haori, and obi cloth are made from a variety of fibers including silk, hemp, cotton, or linen. The cloth was woven in a narrow width, with the yardage varying to the specifics of the garment.

Did You Know?

Cotton Bags

The Textile Bag Manufacturers Association published booklets featuring tips and patterns for the re-purposing of cotton bags that had originally held staples such as flour, salt, feed, sugar, or meal.

Cutter Quilts

Sections or portions of an old quilt can be cut and repurposed into a new item. Cut around any stained, ripped, torn, or frayed sections.

Cutter quilt piece and heart shape

Stash Idea Inspiration

Combine an old or unused block with additional fabrics, yo-yos, buttons, and embroidery.

Find a fun shape, perhaps a pillow or other form, and piece it with left-over scraps of fabric, then add found bits of this and that.

Detail of Denim and Dresden (page 39), vintage feed sack and cotton fabrics, vintage buttons

Buttoned and Zippered UP, 4″ × 9½″ (10.2 × 24.1cm)

Featuring flannel fabrics, vintage tape measure, zipper, celluloid buckle, and variety of celluloid buttons

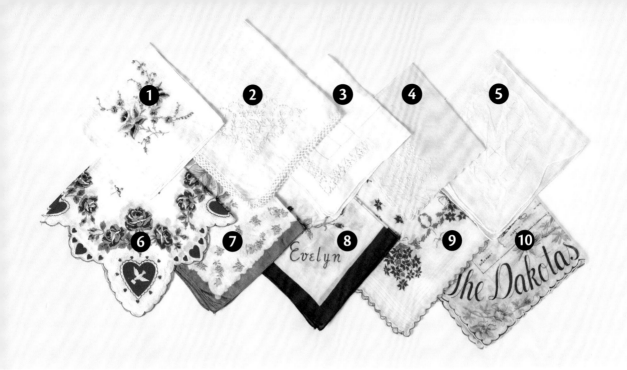

HANKIES AND LINENS

Hankies

Vintage hankies can be layered to create a collage base or can be combined with other fabrics. These are made from cotton, cotton batiste, linen, and silk fabrics.

1–2. Embroidered hankies come in solid white or multi-color patterns.

3–5. Hankies with drawn work, shadow work, or appliqué motifs can have plain or decorative finished edges.

6–7. Printed hankies could have a pattern on one or all four corners or a pattern throughout the square.

8–10. Theme hankies include initials or a signature, holiday images, or reference to a tourist destination.

Note: *Hankies often had a crochet or tatted edge that was worked directly into the edge of the fabric.*

Did You Know?

Souvenir Hankies

Souvenir and signature hankies were often boxed as a single or grouped set, even gift wrapped with a bit of ribbon. I am sure that many husbands and family members found this a brilliant idea for gift-giving occasions.

Linens

Vintage linens of cotton, linen, or silk can be combined to create a collage base that can also include other fabrics.

1. Dishtowels come in solid colors or with a printed pattern, which could range from a floral motif, outdoor scene, or souvenir image.

2–3. Doilies and dresser scarves often have a lace edge or a crochet edge worked directly onto the embroidered or printed fabric.

4. Pillowcases with an embroidered pattern at the opening often have additional crochet or lace trims.

5. Tablecloths have a printed or embroidered pattern in the center, all four corners, or throughout the entire cloth.

Did You Know?

During the last century, the notions department of most major department stores carried a wide variety of embroidery and lace-making threads and tools, iron-on transfer designs, and linens with printed embroidery patterns.

Aunt Martha's iron-on patterns have been around for more than 70 years.

Partially embroidered linen, with open edge for lace.

Stash Idea Inspiration

Combine sections of embroidered doilies, hankies, and pillowcases to create a base. Frame with an old embroidery hoop, then adorn with ribbonwork and lace flowers. See Hoop Frame (page 136), and Flowers and Leaves (page 54) for ideas.

Marzipan Confetti, 9½" (24.1cm) in diameter.

Combine an embroidered hanky with scraps of fabric, bits of lace, ribbonwork, and silk ribbon embroidery to create an heirloom keepsake. See Alternate Foundation (page 137).

Cut two hankies into quarters, then layer them to create a small hanging. Embroider and embellish with ribbonwork and buttons. See Scrap Pins (page 133).

For Elizabeth, 7¼" (18.4cm) in diameter.

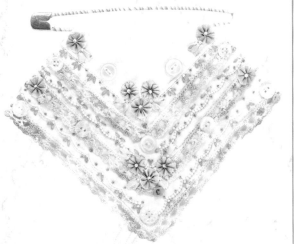

Hankies and Rosettes, 7" × 5¾" (17.8 × 14.6cm).

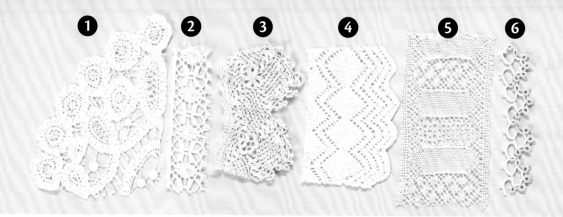

LACE

Hand-Made Laces

Vintage lace can be used for embellishment and is made from cotton, linen, or silk threads.

1. Battenberg lace is created with a combination of special woven tapes that are basted to a paper design and connected with a pattern of buttonhole stitches worked with needle and thread.

2. Bobbin lace is created by twisting and crossing bobbins, wound with fine thread, over and around a pattern of pins stuck into a small pillow form.

3. Crochet lace is made with a crochet hook, forming a series of connected loops into a pattern using thread. Popular styles include squared-off filet crochet and Irish crochet, with 3-D elements.

4. Knitted lace is made with fine knitting needles, working a variety of stitches into a pattern using thread.

5. Needle lace is created by basting outlining threads to a paper pattern, then stitching a pattern of buttonhole stitches with a needle and thread.

6. Tatted lace is made by looping thread—wound around a small shuttle—over the hand, moving the shuttle in and out of the loop into a series of knots and picots.

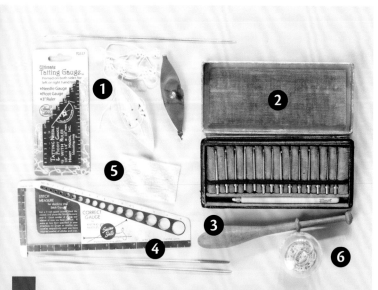

Lace-making tools

1. Tatting shuttles, needle, gauge

2. Crochet hook set

3. Bobbin

4. Knitting needles, gauge

5. Sharps and tapestry needles used for needle lace

6. Thread holder

Stash Idea Inspiration

Collage a piece of vintage upholstery linen or other fabric with your stashed bits of lace, add in silk ribbon embroidery stitches, and now you have a new treasure. See Embroidery and Embellishment Stitches (page 70).

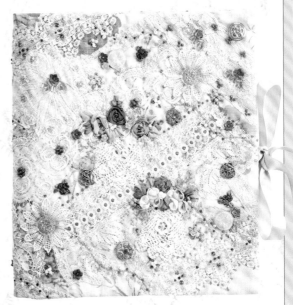

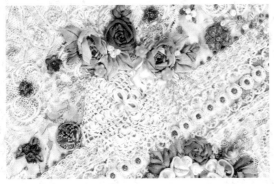

Silk embroidered roses bloom in a basket made from Irish crochet lace.

Lace and Rose Finery Book Cover, front view, covered with beautiful bits of exquisite vintage lace.

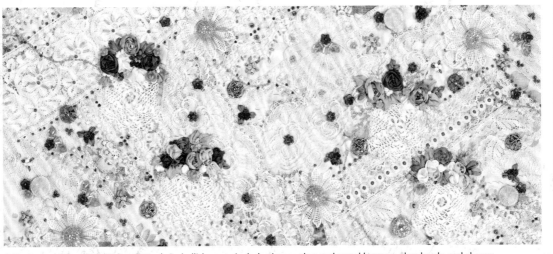

Full exterior, 19″ × 10½″ (48.3 × 26.7cm). Embellishments include vintage glass and metal buttons, glass beads, and charms.

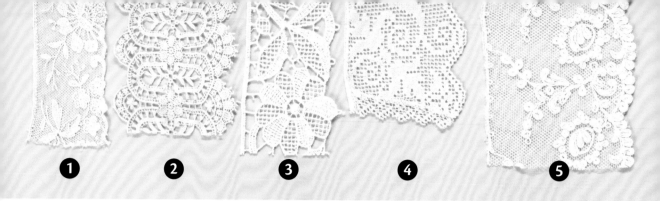

Machine-Made Laces

Machine-made laces are made from cotton, linen, or synthetic threads.

1. Bobbin lace is woven on machines that reproduce the net and solid areas by carrying threads from the more solid areas across the back, which are then clipped off.

2. Chemical lace is a machine-embroidered pattern worked onto a stabilizing fabric. The stabilizer is dissolved with a chemical or burned away with heat, leaving only the stitched pattern.

3. Needle lace is a type of chemical lace. It often has distinctive bars connecting the more solid design elements and usually has a heavier thread outlining the designs.

4. Net darning is worked with an ecru-colored thread that is heavier than other machine-made lace. The design is worked into a woven mesh of squares and solid designs.

5. Tambour work or Limerick-style lace is usually embroidered on net, with machine stitches that look like straight or chain stitches.

Types of Lace

1. Beading trims have regularly spaced openings throughout the length, to insert a ribbon or cord.

2. Edging lace has one straight edge and one scalloped edge.

3. Eyelet or whitework lace has an embroidered design on cotton fabric with one unfinished edge.

4. Galloon lace has scalloped details on both edges.

5. Insertion lace has two straight edges, which can be sewn to a piece of fabric that is clipped away to show the openwork section of the lace.

Did You Know?

Machine-Made Lace

Machines that produced lace date back as early as 1589 in England, with the first being a simple knitting machine. Later machines were developed to imitate bobbin lace, Chantilly lace, Tambour work, and embroidery.

The Magic of Variegated and Ombré Threads

Variegated and ombré crochet, tatting, and cotton floss threads have been popular through many eras. These vivid candy-colored items are a fine example of how magical these combinations of color can be.

Vivid variegated crochet items

Repurposing Finery

Finished items such as doilies, collars, and cuffs can be used as a focal point or combined with other components.

Doilies, appliqués, and realistic trims

Gloves, hankies, collars, and cuffs

Storage Tip A sachet of dried lavender or cedar kept close by (but not touching the fibers) will help to protect your treasures from moths and unwanted visitors.

RIBBONS, TRIMS, AND TAPES

Vintage ribbons, trims, and tapes were made in both natural and synthetic fibers and can be used for embellishment.

Ribbons

1. Double-sided satin ribbon has a shiny finish on both sides of the ribbon. It can be one color or two, one on either side.

2. Grosgrain ribbon has a woven pattern of a raised thread that runs through the width of the ribbon. Petersham grosgrain has a scalloped selvage edge created during the weaving process.

3. Jacquard refers to the complex overshot pattern of the threads that are woven to resemble an embroidered pattern.

4. Novelty prints, checks, and stripe patterns are either woven during construction or painted or printed on afterward.

5. Picot-edge ribbon has a loop on one or both selvage edges, which is created through the weaving process.

6. Single-sided satin ribbon has one shiny side and one dull side.

7. Taffeta ribbon has a fine, tight, even weave. Often the warp and weft are two different colors, which create a changeable color on the surface.

8. Velvet ribbon has a plush finish on one side and a flat finish on the other side.

Did You Know?

Ribbons in Style

Rococo fashion was known for excessively elaborate designs that were lavishly trimmed in wide ribbons, large bows, beautiful lace, and elegant flowers. During the Depression era, ribbons and ribbonwork were used to update fashion items such as hats and clothing and home accessories such as clothes hangers and lingerie bags.

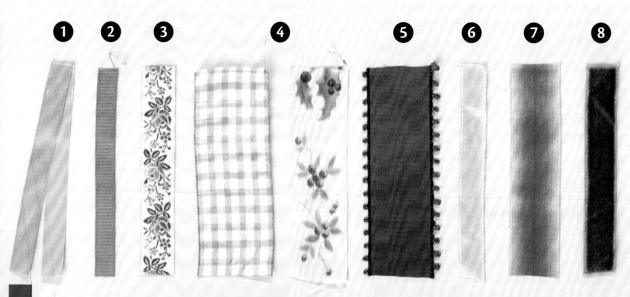

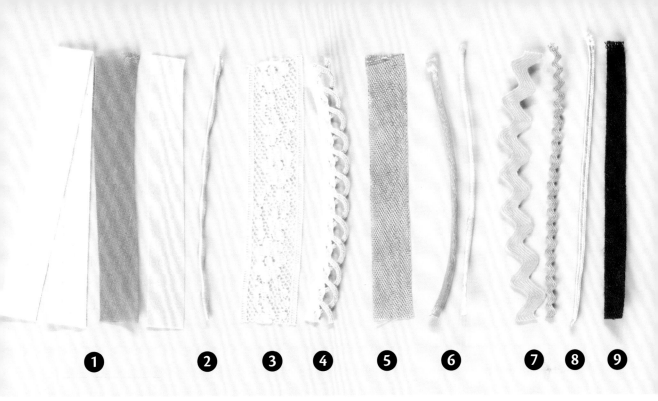

1 2 3 4 5 6 7 8 9

Trims and Tapes

1. Bias hem tape made from cotton, silk, or synthetic fibers comes in a variety of widths, both single and double folded. The raw edges are folded under and permanently pressed.

2. Coronation cord has a pattern that varies from thin to thick.

3. Lace seam binding has a woven selvage edge and comes in a variety of widths.

4. Loop braid has a flat edge, with loops of trim added to one selvage.

5. Rayon hem tape has woven selvages and is tightly woven, yet soft to the touch.

6. Rayon cord comes in two sizes: rattail and mousetail.

7. Rickrack is woven with a curved wave shape on both edges.

8. Soutache braid is thin with a channel running down the center.

9. Twill tape is thick cotton with a subtle woven pattern.

Did You Know?

Rickrack

Waved crochet braid was invented in the mid-nineteenth century. Now known as rickrack, rick rack, zigzag or zig-zag braid, it is made on a braiding machine that interlaces several threads together, with the waved edge formed by varying the tension. The trim is measured by the distance between the top wave (zig) and bottom wave (zag).

Did You Know?

Trims In Fashion

During the mid-twentieth century and to this day, you can find inexpensive jewelry made from rickrack. Usually, you see this simple flower, with stamens or beads for the center.

Rickrack and coronation cords were often combined in crochet and tatting patterns to create trims, doilies, and other items.

Vintage pin and earrings made from rickrack

Vintage pink tatted purse with coronation cord and a silk taffeta lining

Cigarette Silks

Various tobacco companies included small pieces of fabric or ribbon, known as cigarette or tobacco silks, in their product packaging. These collectible items were printed with images of actors and actresses, flags, birds, florals, and other subjects.

Stash Idea Inspiration

Small lengths of wide ribbon can be turned into a pocket or purse. See the Treasure Keeper Pocket (page 135).

Purple Velvet Bag with Violet Gardens pin, 3″ × 3½″ (7.6 × 8.9cm) velvet; Pink Flower Reticule, 2½″ × 2¾″ (6.4 × 7cm) ombré taffeta.

EMBROIDERY THREADS AND RIBBONS

Vintage floss, perle cotton, and sewing threads may come in slightly different colors than their contemporary counterparts but can be used in the same ways.

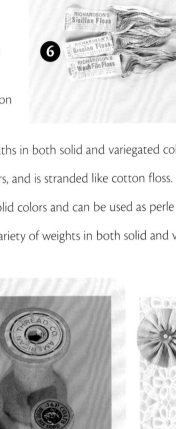

1. Buttonhole twist is a tightly-wound silk thread that comes in solid colors and can be used as perle cotton.

2. Cotton floss comes in a 6-strand skein in solid, ombré, and variegated colors.

3. Rococo trims are woven into a pattern using silk embroidery ribbons.

4. Sewing threads come in cotton and silk wound on wooden or cardboard spools.

5. Silk embroidery ribbons come in a variety of widths in both solid and variegated colors.

6. Silk floss has a shiny surface, comes in solid colors, and is stranded like cotton floss.

7. Silk perle is a twisted silk thread that comes in solid colors and can be used as perle cotton.

8. Tatting and crochet cotton threads come in a variety of weights in both solid and variegated colors.

Did You Know?

Wooden Spools

The wooden spools in your stash could date anywhere from 50–100 years or older. The oldest are etched with the manufacturer's information; newer ones have a paper sticker.

Embroidery Tip Wash your hands frequently and avoid wearing hand lotion or perfume to eliminate the transfer of any oils that could discolor your work while you are stitching.

BUTTONS

Vintage buttons are made from both natural and man-made materials and can be used as embellishments.

Button Materials

1. Ceramic and porcelain buttons are made from a variety of clays fired at varying temperatures and include china and Satsuma.

2. Composition buttons are made from a mixture of materials that produce a random color pattern.

3. Fiber buttons are made from a variety of threads or cords woven or stitched together and formed around a metal, plastic, or wood base.

4. Glass buttons are made by pressing a heated glass rod into a mold or are hand-blown.

5. Jet buttons are carved from lignite, a form of coal that is considered a gemstone.

6. Metal buttons are made from brass, copper, gold, pewter, or sterling.

7–9. Plastic buttons including Bakelite, celluloid, and Lucite are made from a variety of natural and man-made materials. Celluloid is a lightweight plastic, Bakelite is heavy plastic, and acrylics like Lucite fall somewhere in between.

10. Rubber buttons are made from the sap of a rubber tree, which has been vulcanized (hardened).

11. Shell buttons are carved from the outer protective shell of a variety of mollusks.

12. Tagua nut, often referred to as vegetable ivory, is a hard nut that can be carved and dyed.

13. Wood buttons are carved from a variety of soft and hardwoods.

14. Additional materials include antler horn, leather, and animal bone.

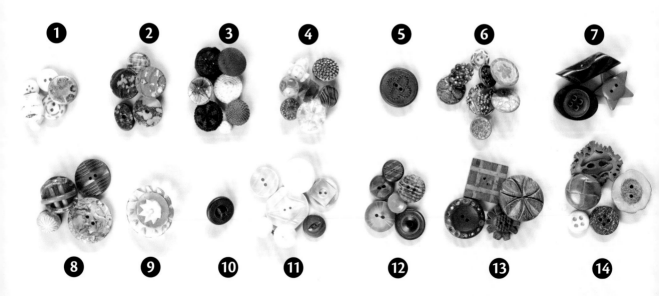

Did You Know?

Celluloid Attributes

Celluloid was such a versatile medium. It could be molded, stamped, extruded, machine-tooled, hollow blown, and more. It could be tinted, or color could be added after the button was formed. These buttons came in a variety of styles, ranging from fanciful creations to imitations of natural materials such as wood or ivory.

Novelty Buttons

Novelty-shaped buttons such as teacups, hats, animals, fruit, flowers, and other items were first made during the mid-1930s and are referred to as realistic or goofy buttons. They were made from a variety of materials and usually sold in sets.

The Button Box

A common household item was a button box, jar, bag, or tin that held all manner of hidden treasures. Buttons removed from old dresses or shirts were tied into strands for safekeeping, along with stray safety pins, sequins, bells, and snaps.

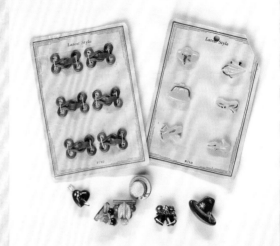

Cards and loose novelty or realistic buttons

Stash Idea Inspiration

Use a length of ribbon or use an old tie as a base to display your favorite buttons.

Deco Drama Necklace, celluloid button styles:

1. Buffed
2. French Ivory
3. Glow bubble
4. Molded
5. Pierced
6. Tight-top

Attachment Styles

SEW-THROUGH BUTTONS

Sew-through buttons are flat or slightly domed, with holes made in the center of the button. These were made in a variety of materials and styles, with the most common number of holes being 2, 3, or 4. Stitch in place with perle cotton or beads.

SHANK BUTTONS

Buttons can have a variety of shank styles, either created at the same time as the button is being formed or, if made separately, often using a different material that was soldered or glued to the back of the button. Stitch in place with perle cotton or sewing thread.

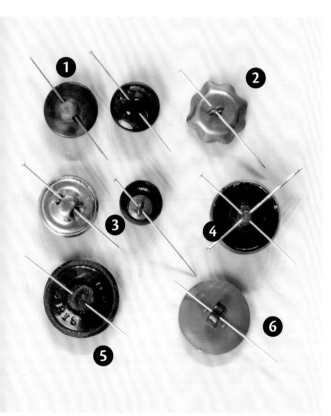

1. A self-shank is carved or molded from the same material as the button while it is being formed.

2. A metal pin shank is attached through a center hole in the middle of the button, with a loop formed on the back.

3. A metal shank with a loop or raised channel is attached to the flat back of a button.

4. A metal box shank has a two-way channel and is attached to the back of a button.

5. Pad-shank buttons, found on fabric buttons, have a metal backplate with a hole in the center that allows the fabric to be pulled through.

6. Plastic buttons that were made from an elaborate mold or unusual shape often had simple celluloid shank glued to the back of the button.

Did You Know?

Button Holes

Machines that drill holes in buttons have a standard spaced pattern. This will allow you to stack and stitch a smaller button on top of a larger button.

Stacked buttons

FREE PROJECTS

For more great ideas on using small bits of your stash, see C&T Publishing's website where you will find a myriad of free projects, including the two below. Go to ctpub.com and click on the link Free Projects.

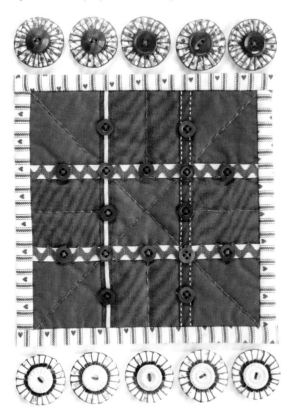

Button Frame, 6½″ × 7″ (16.5 × 17.8cm). Pieces of fabric cover fast2fuse to create a frame that can be embellished with zippers, ribbons, and buttons.

Tic-Tac-Toe Board, 7¾″ × 7¾″ (19.7 × 19.7cm). Stitch pieces of fabric together with trims to create a game board. Use fabric and vintage buttons for game pieces.

1   2   3   4   5

EMBELLISHMENTS AND EPHEMERA

Beads, Sequins, and Charms

Vintage embellishments such as beads, charms, and sequins will add an unexpected touch.

1. Beads can be stitched in place with beading thread.

2. Bells can be stitched in place with perle cotton or beads.

3. Charms, keys, and old coins can be stitched in place with perle cotton or beads.

4. Sequins can be stitched in place with cotton floss or beads.

5. Souffle or Gelatin pieces can be stitched in place with beads.

Old Jewelry

Vintage jewelry parts can add that personal touch to a project. Stitch these in place as you would a button, bead, or charm.

1. Cufflinks: Break apart the components and use the various parts.

2. Earrings, clip back: Remove the metal clip and stitch the earring in place using the holes in the finding.

3. Earrings, screw back: Clip off the metal close to the screw, then curve the remaining metal piece into a loop with a pair of pliers.

4. Necklaces: Break apart the components and use the various parts.

5. Pins: Use the existing pin or remove the pin-back and glue a button finding or flat-back button to the back.

6. Stick pins or tie pins: Couch over the long pin, or remove the pin then glue a button finding to the back.

7. Watch parts and other broken bits of jewelry: Stitch in place at any opening or bar.

1   2   3   5   7   4   6

Did You Know?

Sequin Glamour

Rhinestone and paste jewelry have been popular throughout many eras, none more so than the 1920s, also known as the Roaring Twenties. During this period, sequins were a poor girl's substitute for that sparkle and glitz.

Vintage jewelry made from sequins and beads

Stash Idea Inspiration

Turn old jewelry into new adornments.

1. A metal chain bracelet with grape-shaped buttons attached with jump rings.

2. A bracelet blank with vintage earrings and a pin glued to each blank.

3. A bracelet base made from vintage watches connected with jump rings, and with cufflinks attached with more jump rings.

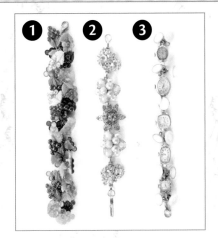

1. A vintage buckle becomes the base for a pin, with glued-on buttons and earrings.

2. A vintage pin frame with a fabric circle (page 66) covered in lace for the center becomes a base for small embellishments.

3. A vintage fur clip used for a pin.

Tip

· If the back of an earring or pin has an uneven surface, glue a piece of felt to the back first, then glue the felt to the surface.

· To use a fur clip or tie tack as a pin, attach a small piece of felt to the tines so they won't damage your clothing.

Sewing Notions

Stitch or glue vintage sewing notions to a project to add that personal touch.

1. Buckles: Stitch in place with perle cotton or beads or thread a piece of ribbon through the buckle and stitch in place.

2. Cloth tape measures or clothing labels: Hand- or machine-sew to a project.

3. Dome snaps, hook and eye closures, and safety pins: Stitch in place with perle cotton or beads.

4. Metal and wooden button forms: Use to create one-of-a-kind buttons.

5. Metal and nylon zippers: Use as a trim or sew into a flower. Use the zipper pull as a charm.

6. Metal or plastic thimbles: Drill a hole through the top or side of the thimble, then stitch in place by hand.

7. Sewing machine bobbins: Hand stitch in place through the holes.

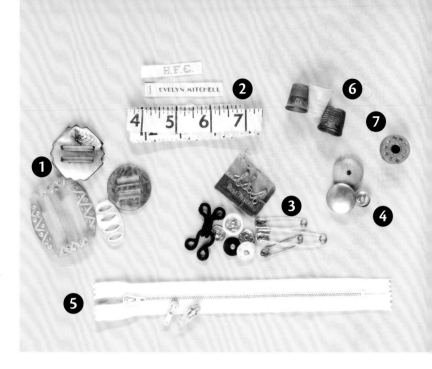

Stash Idea Inspiration

Knot buttons onto a length of waxed linen to create a necklace. Glue buttons onto a bracelet base, with zipper pulls attached for charms. Attach notions to a pair of sewing machine bobbins to create a unique pair of earrings.

Chain, Chain, Chain necklace, bracelet, and earrings

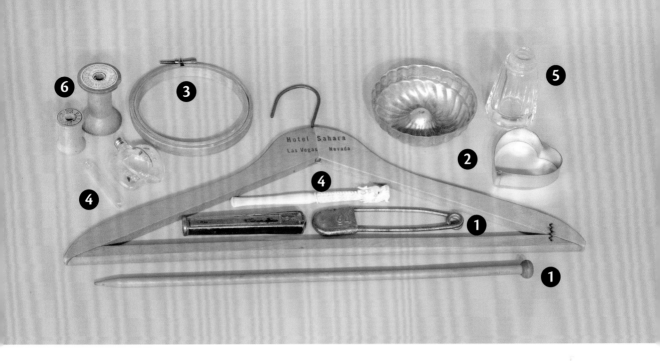

ATTIC, GARAGE, AND JUNK DRAWER FINDS

Look through the stash of stuff hidden in your sewing room, kitchen, or garage for unused and forgotten items.

1. Knitting needles, large laundry safety pins, and wooden hangers: Use to hang a project on the wall.

2. Metal cookie cutter and aspic molds: Can be used for a variety of items.

3. Metal and wooden embroidery hoops: Use to frame an embroidered project.

4. Perfume bottles or vials, knife handles, and cigarette holders: Stitch to a project or use as a pin.

5. Small bottles, saltshakers, or ink wells: Use as vases.

6. Wooden spools: Use for ornaments, vases, or embellishments.

Which Glue to Use? Glue objects that cannot be sewn onto the surface of the project.

· Use an adhesive like E6000 to glue glass, ceramic, or metal to these same materials.

· Fabric glue, fabric glue sticks, or spray adhesive can glue one fiber to another fiber.

· Hot or low-temp glue can glue wood, plastic, or fiber to these same materials.

Note: Work in a well-ventilated area when using any type of glue.

Detail of Cotton Candy and Cinnamon Hearts featuring cigarette holders used for flower vases.

Stash Idea Inspiration

String wooden spools onto florist wire to create a base for a wreath. Embellish with ribbonwork flowers, buttons, and other ephemera. See Flowers and Leaves (page 54).

Spools and Tools, 8″ × 5¾″ (20.3 × 14.6cm)

Orphaned or found items can be turned into small vases, like this vintage glass saltshaker and ink well. See Vase of Flowers (page 139) and Altering the Past (page 47) for ideas.

Impromptu vases

Turn a collection of aluminum cookie molds wrapped with ribbon into a wreath. Embellish with ribbonwork flowers, buttons, and other ephemera. See Flowers and Leaves (page 54).

Cookie Cutter Wreath, 9½″ × 11″, (24.1 × 27.9cm)

An old wooden clothes hanger, laundry pin, or knitting needle can be a unique way to hang a project. See Custom Hanger (page 101) and Which Glue to Use? (page 37) for ideas.

Detail of Into the Garden (page 47)

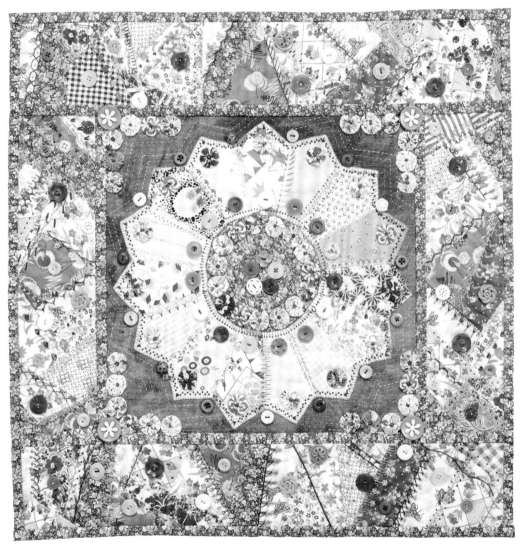

Treasure Hunting

Denim and Dresden, 23¼″ × 23½″ (59.1 × 59.7cm)

The Dresden Plate block, purchased at a thrift store for $1.00, was originally sewn to a piece of muslin and embroidered with black floss. The embroidery and background were removed and replaced with a denim square and a border of crazy-pieced feed sack and cotton print fabrics. See Stitching Creatively (page 89) and Embroidery and Embellishment Stitches (page 70) for ideas.

WHERE TO FIND THE GOOD STUFF

You never know what you are going to find, especially if you peruse with an open mind and think outside the box. Just let the muse take you along her merry journey.

Scouting Out Local Sources

There is nothing like seeing the item up-close-and-personal. A great resource for all things old and new may be just a few blocks from home.

- Antique shows are often held once or twice a year at your local convention hall.

- Church-run charity and thrift stores are stocked with donations that will include a broad variety of items ranging from new to several decades old.

- Flea markets and swap meets offer a broad range of items. Depending on the organization, these can be held every weekend, once a month, or once a year. Look for ones that specialize in the vintage items that you are interested in.

- Garage sales and estate sales in your local area can often offer a surprise or two.

- National charities such as the Salvation Army and Goodwill have a broad range of donated items from both private and commercial sectors. Items that have a greater value may be sectioned off in a "boutique area" or offered through their eBay store.

- Quilt guilds, button clubs, and other specialty organizations often sponsor a special sale for their members that allow them to sell their "own stash" and may also include local retailers.

SAVVY IN-PERSON SHOPPING TIPS

- Arrive early when shopping flea market, antique show, or estate sales.

- Bring a tape measure, your reading glasses, a tote bag, a notepad, and a pencil.

- Small bills and coins are always helpful.

- Buying multiple items from one vendor may help you to negotiate a better price. Be mindful and honest when negotiating.

Quantities

This depends on how much is available and what you can afford. Vintage items are essentially finite in nature, meaning they won't be made again! If you see something that you like, want, or need, chances are someone else may also fancy it! I suggest that you buy what you can, otherwise at some point, you will be asking yourself with regret, "Why didn't I buy that?"

GATHERING GUIDELINES FOR A 10˝ × 10˝ (25.4 × 25.4CM) WALLHANGING

- Large component: 1 doily, cuff, or appliqué that could be used as a center design.

- Medium components: 3–5 groups containing 4–5 similar items such as large buttons, small appliqués, or ribbonwork flowers.

- Small components: 3–5 groups containing 10–15 similar items such as small buttons, charms, or other embellishments.

Conferences and Conventions

Investigate national shows that may include specialty exhibits, vendors, or classes. Some of the organizations have local chapters.

On-Line Resources

On-line resources like eBay and Etsy offer a wide variety of both raw goods and finished items.

MAKING AN EDUCATED PURCHASE

Defining a treasure can be complicated. Does the term treasure mean that it is one of a kind, the right color, found in an unexpected place, or a great deal? That depends on you and the circumstances in which you found it.

What is Something Worth?

- Price vs. value: The price of an item is determined by the seller; the value of the item is determined by how much the buyer will pay for the item. You must decide for yourself what price you consider fair.

- Determining the age: Look for colors, styles, and designs that would have come from a specific era. The words vintage and antique can be confusing descriptions; make sure you know how these terms relate to the seller's description of the item for sale.

- Condition: Look for new unused items, NOS (new out-of-stock), or barely used items that require a slight cleaning or pressing. You don't want to take on more work than is necessary to use the item.

- Quality: Look for items that are made from good materials. These items will hold up the best when you are incorporating them into your creations.

- Rare vs. common: Do your homework—research prices while shopping for specific items and expect that rare items will cost more than commonly found ones.

- Do you like It? If you answer *Yes* to this question, then the points above may not apply. Enjoy that treasure without regrets!

Stash Idea Inspiration

This entire collection of doilies, napkins, and small serving placemats was given to me by friends and family members. The kid glove belonged to my grandmother, and my mother stitched the oval floral pieces. The earrings came from my husband's grandmothers and the jacquard ribbon from his mother. The vintage buttons, jewelry, perfume vials, and glass beads were purchased at thrift stores and online. See Lace, Doilies, and Appliqués (page 96), and Flowers and Leaves (page 54) for ideas.

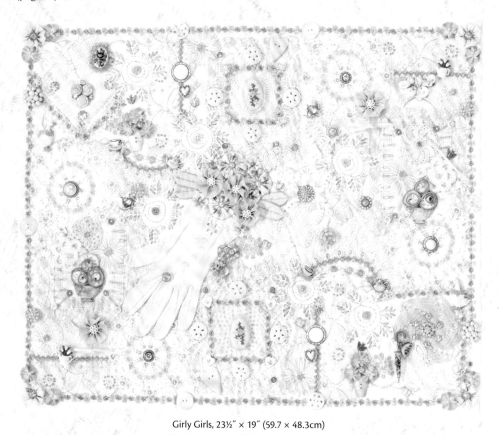

Girly Girls, 23½" × 19" (59.7 × 48.3cm)

A Note from the Author

Never look at a gift as anything but a wonderful gesture. Chances are that you will be able to find a special place for that treasure, and when you look at it you will think of the person who gave it to you. I know that I do, and I extend my heartfelt thanks to every one of you that gave me a special gift from your heart!

MIXING THE OLD WITH THE NEW

Look for colors that are used throughout the eras—reds, pinks, yellows, blues, greens, browns, tans, and creams. Often the shading will be slightly off, but you can find ways to blend these with newer components.

Some projects come together easily, such as the following two examples. Others such as Madame Butterfly (page 14), took me years to gather all the components together.

My Fair Lady

This small, framed print combines new fabrics with old trims and buttons in hues of pink, green, and cream.

- 1900–1940: Wavy pink and white trim, mother-of-pearl buttons, glass buttons, pink glass hexagon beads, sequins, pink ombré silk embroidery ribbon.

- 2000–2010: Floral fabric, floral bridal appliqués, green silk embroidery ribbon, reproduction print cigarette silk (center).

- New: Green satin ribbon, cotton lace, glass seed beads, cotton floss, perle cotton.

My Fair Lady, 8″ × 10″ (20.3 × 25.4cm)

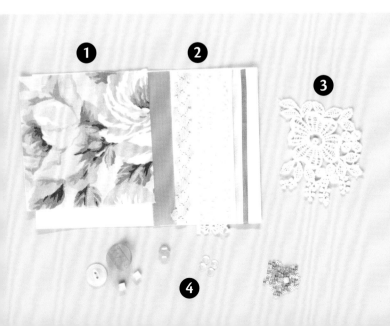

1. Fabric
2. trims and ribbons
3. appliqué
4. embellishments

Cotton Candy and Cinnamon Hearts

The center embroidery of this wallhanging is combined with both new and old fabrics, trims, laces, and buttons, concentrating on reds, pinks, greens, and neutrals.

- 1930–1950: Feed sack fabrics in red and cream, Swiss dot fabric, red-and-white-striped fabric, embroidered cotton trims, satin and ombré ribbons, buttons, novelty cigarette holders, plastic thimbles, advertising buttons, beads

- 1960–1995: Embroidered heart (center) made by my mom, jacquard ribbons, pink-and-white heart fabric, ladybug pin

- New: Red and pink with print fabric, satin, check and grosgrain ribbons, lace, perle cotton, cotton floss, buttons, plastic charms, glass bead

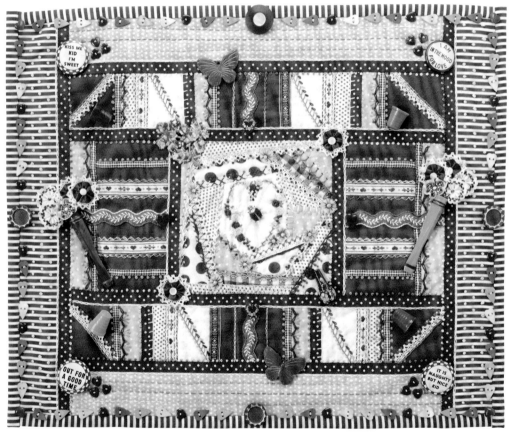

Cotton Candy and Cinnamon Hearts, 18¾" × 15" (47.6 × 38.1cm)

Fabrics   Trims

TAKING CARE OF YOUR TREASURES

Cleaning

Group like colors of fabric, linen, or lace. Use hot water for white and neutral colors, warm water for bright colors, and cold water for dark colors.

1. Fill a tub full of water, add the cleaning product, and swish the water.

2. Place the materials in the water, making sure there is room for the pieces to move around.

3. Soak the items for 25–30 minutes, then RINSE well.

4. If the water is still dirty, repeat the wash-and-soak process.

5. Hang dry over a plastic hanger or machine dry on low heat.

6. To press, use distilled water in a spray bottle and iron. Spray the item first, then press with a clean iron on the appropriate setting.

Note: *For fabrics, try Oxiclean or Biz. For delicate items, try Restoration Linen Cleaner or Mama's Miracle Linen Soak.*

MATERIAL SPECIFICS

- Fabric: Hand or machine wash, hang dry or machine dry on low heat, press.

- Laces, ribbons, and trims: Hand wash, hang dry. To press, gently pass the lace or ribbon over the warm plate of an upright iron.

- Embroidery threads: Wash in a mild soap, hang dry.

- Buttons, charms, or sequins: Clean with a soft cloth. Use water sparingly and never on metal.

WORKING AROUND ISSUES

- Food, beverage, and blood stains are difficult to remove. Cut around or cover the stain with lace, ribbons, or trims.

- Rips and holes in vintage fabrics, linens, and lace are difficult to repair. Instead, cut around or cover the section with a piece of ribbon, appliqué, or button.

- Permanent folds in hankies, linens, and other fabrics are a sign that the fibers are breaking down. The folds cannot be removed. Cut around the section or cover with a piece of ribbon or lace.

- Rust stains in fabric left from a metal pin cannot be removed; unfortunately the fiber will continue to deteriorate. Cut around or cover the section with a piece of ribbon, appliqué, or button.

Use embroidered appliqués, buttons, yo-yos, or ribbonwork flowers to cover small holes.

Determining Fiber Content

An easy way to determine if the fiber is natural or synthetic is to pull a thread from the cut edge. If it is natural, the thread will pull easily away from the weave. If it is synthetic, the fiber will look fuzzy and will be harder to pull away.

The fiber content can further be determined by burning a small section of the fiber with a candle. Have a small bowl of water handy and work on a ceramic surface like your kitchen countertop.

- Cotton will rapidly take to the flame and will continue to burn. The odor smells like paper.

- Linen will take longer to burn than cotton. The odor smells like rope.

- Rayon will rapidly take to the flame. The odor smells like paper or rags.

- Silk will slowly take the flame, will sputter, and usually self-extinguish; the odor smells like hair.

- Synthetic fibers will rapidly take to the flame and bead up. The odor will have a chemical smell.

- Wool will slowly take to the flame and will self-extinguish; the odor smells like hair.

Storage

Clean items before storing with other items, as odors can transfer. Remove any rubber bands, pins, or tape that may be attached to fabric, laces, ribbons, or trims.

- Fabric, linens, lace, and appliqués: Store in a plastic or cardboard box with acid-free tissue paper.

- Loose ribbons, trims, and lace: Wrap into a loop or a figure-eight bundle and store in a plastic bag.

- Packaged ribbons and trims: Store the original spool or piece of cardboard in a plastic or cardboard box.

- Embroidery threads and ribbon: Store in a plastic bag by color or by project.

- Buttons: Store plastic in a cardboard box; store shell, glass, metal, nut, and wood in a plastic bag or container.

- Beads, sequins, and charms: Store in a plastic bag or container.

Harvesting Tips Beads and sequins can be harvested from frayed bits of fabric or appliqués to be re-purposed and given a new life.

Altering the Past

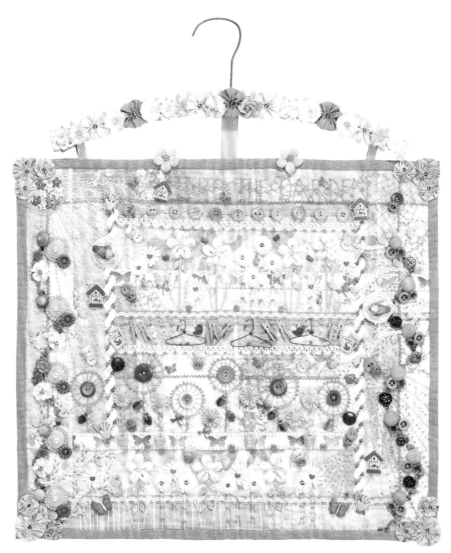

Into the Garden, 20¼˝ × 18˝ (51.4 × 45.7cm)

This randomly patch- and strip-pieced base of upholstery and linen fabrics is hand-quilted, embroidered, and embellished with an eclectic mixture of old and new ribbons, trims, threads, buttons, and beads. It is attached to an old wooden hanger adorned with ribbonwork and other pieces of ephemera that can be found in this chapter. See Custom Hanger (page 101), and Which Glue to Use? (page 37) for ideas.

GATHERED BITS AND PIECES

Now that you have your stash of treasures gathered, you may be asking yourself what can I make with the little bits? Within this chapter, you will find instructions on how to dye, sew, or stitch these pieces into one-of-a-kind embellishments that will be unique to your stash and your projects.

Detail of Sweet Dreams (page 150). See Decorative Trims (page 62) and Flowers and Leaves (page 54) for how to get creative with trims.

Detail of Patched and Buttoned (page 64). See Decorative Trims (page 62) and Little Stitched Extras (page 65) for how to create one-of-a-kind embellishments.

Detail of Butterfly Fields (page 151). See Dyeing to be Beautiful (page 49) for how to dye your ribbons, and Flowers and Leaves (page 54) for how to sew a variety of ribbonwork flowers.

Detail of Notions of Spring (page 61). See Flowers and Leaves (page 54) for how to sew a variety of ribbonwork flowers from your vintage notions.

DYEING TO BE BEAUTIFUL

I use Colorhue Dyes for natural fibers such as cotton, linen, rayon, silk, and wool. These dyes are very concentrated and the dye absorbs and sets instantly, with no additional chemicals needed to set the color. These dyes are non-toxic and the remaining dye can be poured down the drain with no worries to the environment.

Note: *These dyes react best with 100% natural fibers, with silk taking the dye the strongest, and cotton taking the dye with less intense saturation. If you are not using RTD (ready to dye fibers), then you will need to prewash everything that you will be dyeing.*

Supplies and Tools

COLORHUE DYES

Colorhue dyes include rose, yellow, blue, turquoise, brown, green, black, goldenrod, eggplant, and pumpkin. To mix your own colors see Mixing Colors (page 50), use rose for red; yellow or goldenrod for yellow; and blue or turquoise for blue.

SETTING UP

- Wear a protective covering over your clothes and use plastic gloves.

- Cover the work surface with a plastic cloth and arrange the dyes and other tools.

- Have plenty of water and paper towels on hand.

- Use clean, unused clear plastic cups and measuring spoons for water and dyes.

- Use glass or plastic eyedroppers/pipettes to measure dye amounts.

  Note: *Do not use any metal containers or utensils.*

Fill 3 containers with water (room temperature) and label them for these purposes:

- Pre-wet before dyeing

- Rinse water for pipettes

- Rinse water for fibers after dye bath

Dyeing

1. Wet each fiber thoroughly and wring until no water drips from it.

2. Immerse the fiber directly into the dye bath, and swish the liquid to disperse the dye. Hold the fiber in place with a pipette for a few minutes.

3. Rinse the fiber in the plastic cup, swishing for a few seconds. Repeat until the water is clear.

4. Place the wet fiber on a paper towel to dry.

Note: *The dye will dry several shades lighter in color than it was when wet.*

Colorhue Dyes

Mixing Colors

1. Mix each dye bath into a separate plastic cup according to the chart below.

Note: *If you are using any color directly from the bottle, place 20 drops of dye into the plastic cup.*

COLOR RECIPES

Color / Warm or cool color	Use this many drops
Red/warm	20 drops
Red-orange/warm	15 drops red and 5 drops yellow
Orange/warm	10 drops each of red and yellow
Yellow-orange/warm	15 drops yellow and 5 drops red
Yellow/warm	20 drops
Yellow-green/cool	15 drops yellow and 5 drops blue
Green/cool	10 drops each of yellow and blue
Blue-green/cool	15 drops blue and 5 drops yellow
Blue/cool	20 drops
Blue-violet/cool	15 drops blue and 5 drops red
Violet/cool	10 drops each of blue and red
Red-violet/warm	15 drops red and 5 drops blue

2. Add in the water according to the Dye to Water Formulas (below).

Note: *If you need a larger dye bath, determine the amount of water needed first, then multiply the drops of dye according to the formulas.*

DYE TO WATER FORMULA

Desired effect	Dye/water ratio
Intense	20 drops dye to 1 tablespoon water
Medium	20 drops dye to 3 tablespoons water
Light	20 drops dye to 5 tablespoons water

RUSTIC AGING

For an antiqued look, use a brown dye bath. Use the brown dye or create your own dye bath by mixing one of the following formulas into a cup. Add in 6 tablespoons of water.

- 10 drops each of red and green
- 10 drops each of yellow and violet
- 10 drops each of blue and orange

SADDENED COLORS

You can add black and brown dyes directly to the dye baths created from the Color Recipes. Add 5 drops of black to cool colors or 5 drops of brown to warm colors.

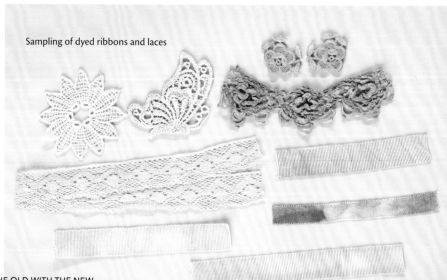

Sampling of dyed ribbons and laces

Stash Idea Inspiration

Hand-dye a linen napkin or tablecloth and use as a base for an embroidery design.

Hand-dye a vintage lace cuff for a basket and fill it with cotton grosgrain ribbonwork flowers and vintage buttons. See Lace, Doilies, and Appliqués (page 96) for ideas.

Morris Gardens, 11″ × 11″ (27.9 × 27.9cm), dyed base using a saddened green dye

Flowers in a Cuff, 9½″ × 9½″ (24.1 × 24.1cm)

Create a brooch with ribbonwork flowers made from hand-dyed ribbons and embellished vintage mother-of-pearl buttons. See the option under fabric circle (page 66) and Flowers and Leaves (page 54) for ideas.

Dyed Posies Brooch, 3″ (7.6cm) in diameter

RIBBON AND TRIM DETAILS

Glossary of Hand-Sewn Stitches

For hand sewing, use a small sharps needle and sewing thread, single strand (unless otherwise noted), and knot the thread.

Option: *If the directions call for a crinoline base, you can substitute heavy interfacing or Pellon 809 Décor-Bond.*

- Anchor knot: Bring the needle through the selvage edge of the ribbon. Repeat, inserting the needle through the loop that is created; tighten the knot.

- Assembly stitch: A series of short, even stitches used to stitch two pieces together to form a seam.

- Gather stitch: A series of long, even stitches used to gather and form a center or the edge of a component.

- Loop-over: The thread is looped over an edge any time the direction of the gather stitches is changed.

- Tackstitch: A small, straight stitch used to attach the components together.

- Whipstitch: A series of short, angled straight stitches used to attach the components together.

Preventing Frayed Edges

- Synthetic ribbon: Sear the raw edges with a Thread Zap II pen.
- Cotton ribbon: Place a line of Fray Check along the raw edges.

CUTTING LENGTHS

The directions for each ribbonwork flower or leaf include a formula that is multiplied by the ribbon width (RW) of the ribbon you are working with.

Use the chart below to convert inches or millimeters into the decimal equivalent. Multiply that amount by the RW formula given and cut the ribbon to that measurement.

RW (RIBBON WIDTH) CONVERSION CHART

Inch	Millimeter	Decimal equivalent
1"	25mm	1
⅞"	22mm	0.875
¾"	19mm	0.75
⅝"	16mm	0.625
½"	12mm	0.5
⅜"	10mm	0.375
¼"	6mm	0.25

Attaching Ribbons, Lace, and Trims to Fabric

- Lace and appliqués: Hand stitch through the open spaces, trying not to pierce the thread of the lace.

- Ribbons and trims: Hand stitch with a tackstitch every ¼" (6mm), alternating between sides.

- Rickrack trim: Hand stitch with a tackstitch every wave.

- Soutache, rayon, or coronation cords: Hand stitch with the couched stitch (page 74).

- Zippers: Hand stitch in place along the edge with a tackstitch every ¼" (6 mm).

  Note: *To separate a zipper into two pieces, first cut through the bottom edge of the zipper to remove the metal bar, then remove the zipper-pull and split the zipper in half.*

Flower Centers

1. Beads: Use sewing or beading thread.

2. Buttons: Use perle cotton or sewing thread.

3. French knot stitch: Use 4mm silk embroidery ribbon.

Fancy Ribbons

Two-Color Ribbon

1. Cut 1 piece each of the same or different widths of ribbon.

2. Hold the ribbons together, slightly overlapping the inner selvage edges.

3. Machine stitch the selvage edges together with a zigzag stitch.

Layered-Inner-Edge Ribbon

1. Cut 1 piece each of two different widths of ribbon.

2. Pin or use a fabric glue stick to attach the narrower ribbon to a selvage edge of the wider ribbon.

3. Machine or hand stitch along the selvage edges.

Option: *You can substitute a zipper for the wider ribbon, using a narrower ribbon or rickrack trim. Or you can substitute a piece of lace for the narrower ribbon.*

Beaded Lace and Ribbon

Thread a length of ribbon with a bodkin, safety pin, or chenille needle. Thread through the open sections (beading) of the trim; cut off the excess ribbon.

Option: *You can substitute perle cotton or floss for a narrower beaded edge.*

Fancy-Edge Ribbon

1. Cut 1 piece each of ribbon and lace.

2. Machine or hand stitch the lace to a selvage edge of the ribbon.

Ribbon Layered with Lace

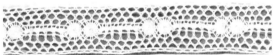

1. Cut 1 length of ribbon and 1 length of lace the same width as the ribbon

2. Pin or use a fabric glue stick to attach the lace to a selvage edge of the ribbon.

3. Hand stitch along the selvage edge.

Flowers and Leaves

See RW (Ribbon Width) Conversion Chart (page 52)

Rosette

1. Cut 1 length of ribbon 8RW.

2. Fold the ribbon length in half, right side in, matching the raw edges. Stitch the raw edges together with a ⅛" (3mm) seam allowance using the assembly stitch.

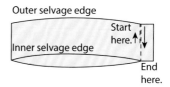

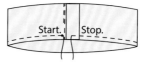

3. Starting at the inner selvage edge next to the seam, gather stitch through 1 layer of ribbon along the continuous selvage edge back to the seam.

4. Gently pull the thread to gather the stitches and form the middle of the flower. Anchor knot the thread into the raw edges.

Posy

1. Cut 1 length of ribbon 8RW.

2. Along the inner selvage edge, mark 1RW from each raw edge. Anchor knot the thread into the outer selvage edge ⅛" (3mm) from the raw edge. Gather stitch at an angle to the mark at the inner selvage edge.

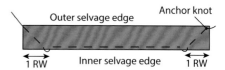

3. Loop over the edge and continue to gather stitch along the selvage edge to the remaining mark. Loop over the edge, then gather stitch at an angle to the outer selvage edge, ⅛" (3mm) from the raw edge.

4. Stitch through the selvage edge next to the beginning anchor knot. Gently pull the thread to gather the center of the flower. Match the right sides of the raw edges. Anchor knot the thread into the raw edges.

Fancy Flowers

Posy

Rosette

1. Cut 1 length of ribbon 8RW, using the new width created by any one of the Fancy Ribbon suggestions (page 53).

2. Follow Steps 2–4 for either the rosette or posy (page 54).

Fuller Flowers

Posy

Rosette

1. Cut 1 length of lace or rayon hem tape 12RW–16RW.

2. Follow Steps 2–4 for either the posy or rosette (page 54).

Crinkly Flowers

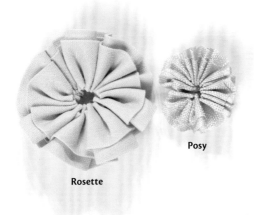

Posy

Rosette

1. Cut 1 length of double-fold bias tape or rayon tape 8RW–12RW. Fold the width of the ribbon almost in half, with the back edge higher than the front edge.

2. Follow Steps 2–4 for either the rosette or posy (page 54), with the fold as the inner edge.

Frilly Flowers

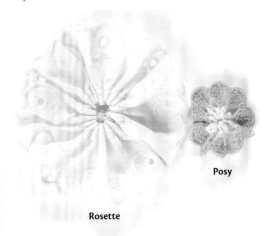

Posy

Rosette

1. Cut 1 length of eyelet or fancy edge trim 10RW.

2. Follow Steps 2–4 for either the rosette or posy (page 54), with the scalloped edge as the outer edge of the flower and the straight edge as the center of the flower.

Note: *If the trim has a raw edge on one end, push this back to the wrong side of the flower as you gather in the center.*

Double Rosette

1. Cut 1 length of ribbon 8RW and 1 length 12RW. Cut 1 circle of crinoline 3RW.

Crinoline

2. Using the 8RW length of ribbon, follow the directions for the rosette (page 54). Stitch the center to the crinoline.

3. Using the 12RW length of ribbon, follow the directions for the rosette to Step 3. Place the opening of the second rosette around and under the first rosette.

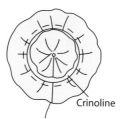

Crinoline

4. Gently pull the thread to gather the stitches around the middle of the first rosette. Anchor knot the thread into the crinoline; tackstitch the inner edge to the crinoline.

Vintage Favorite

1. Cut 1 circle of crinoline 4RW. *Thread a needle with perle cotton and knot the thread. Come up through the center and stitch 5 spokes; knot and cut the thread.

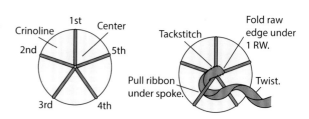

Crinoline · 1st · Center · 2nd · 5th · 3rd · 4th · Tackstitch · Pull ribbon under spoke. · Fold raw edge under 1 RW. · Twist.

2. Cut 1 length of ribbon 75RW plus 2″ (5.1cm). Fold 1 raw edge under 1RW and place over the center of the spokes. Tackstitch onto the center of the circle.

3. Thread the other raw edge into a large-eye needle. Twirl the needle to the right to twist the ribbon. Weave the needle and ribbon over and under the spokes counterclockwise, pulling the ribbon through the spokes.

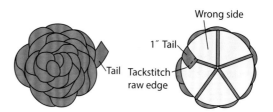

Tail · Wrong side · 1″ Tail · Tackstitch raw edge

4. Cut the ribbon, leaving a 1″ (2.5cm) tail. Tackstitch this to the wrong side of the crinoline.

Rickrack Flower

5-petal

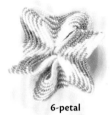

6-petal

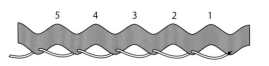

1. Anchor knot the thread into the bottom center of the first wave. Whipstitch through the next 5–6 waves. Cut off the excess trim through the center of the next wave after the last stitch.

2. Stitch through the first wave next to the beginning anchor knot. Gently pull the thread to gather the center of the flower. Match the right sides of the ends.

3. Pull the thread tight. Anchor knot the thread into the ends. Stitch the 2 ends together with tackstitches. Cut off the excess trim close to the stitches.

Rickrack Mum

1. Follow step 1 of the rickrack flower (above), stitching through 15 waves.

2. Gently pull the thread to gather in the petals, folding each consecutive petal over the previous petal.

3. Pull the thread tight. Fold the beginning raw edge under and then over the ending raw edge. Anchor knot the thread into both edges.

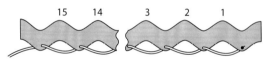

Rickrack Rose

1. Follow the directions for braided rickrack (page 62) using 15" (38.1cm) lengths (or longer). Place a pin in the middle of the braided length.

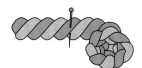

2. Fold 1 end down below the edge of the braid; fold this in half again. Tackstitch in place.

3. Turn and roll the braid into a bud, tackstitching the center of the waves to the wrong side. Repeat this step to the pin.

4. Fan out the remaining petals, tackstitching the waves as in Step 3. Tackstitch the raw edge to the wrong side; anchor knot.

Simple Rose

1. Cut 1 length of lace or rayon hem tape 20RW. Fold the length in half, with the raw edges at the beginning of the flower.

Fold   Raw edges

1 RW

2. Mark 1RW from the raw edges along the inner selvage edges. Anchor knot the thread into the outer selvage edges ⅛" (3mm) from the raw edges. Gather stitch at an angle through both layers to the mark at the inner selvage edge.

3. Loop the thread over the edges and continue to gather through both selvage edges to the fold.

4. Gently pull the thread to gather the center of the flower, with the folded edge on top and the raw edges to the back. Pull the thread tight; anchor knot. Tackstitch the gathered portion; anchor knot the thread.

Rolled Rose

1. Cut 1 length of ribbon 20RW.

2. Fold one end down below the edge of the ribbon; fold this in half again to create a tail. Tackstitch in place.

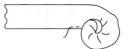

3. Gather stitch 1½" (3.8cm) along the selvage edge. Pull in the gathers, wrapping around the center fold. Tackstitch the gathered portion to the tail.

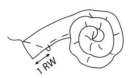

4. Continue to gather stitch every 2" (5.1cm). Tackstitch the gathered portion in a continuous spiral on the wrong side of the flower. Stop 2" (5.1cm) before the edge.

5. Gather stitch to 1RW from the raw edge. *Gather at an angle to ⅛" (3mm) of the raw edge. Tackstitch the remaining gathered portion in a spiral and the raw edge to the wrong side of the flower; anchor knot.

Zipper Rose

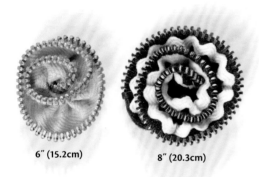

6" (15.2cm)   8" (20.3cm)

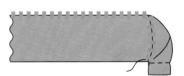

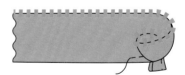

1. Begin with 1 half of a zipper. Cut the length to 6" (15.2cm) or longer.

2. Follow Steps 2 and 3 of the rolled rose (above).

3. Gather stitch every 2" (5.1cm). Tackstitch the gathered portion in a continuous spiral on the wrong side of the flower.

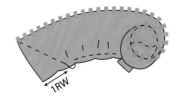

4. Gather stitch the last section, stopping ½" (1.2cm) from the raw edge. Follow Step 5 of the rolled rose from *.

Option: *You can add rickrack trim or other ribbon details to the zipper before you begin stitching.*

Loop Leaf

Option A (4RW)   **Option B (8RW)**

1. Cut 1 length of ribbon 4RW, 6RW, or 8RW and follow either option to the right.

Option A: Fold the length of ribbon in half. Kiss the selvage edges together.

Option B: Overlap the edges of the ribbon.

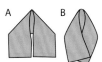

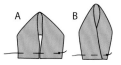

2. Anchor knot the thread at one edge. Gather stitch across and ⅛" (3mm) above the raw edges. Pull the thread to gather the stitches; anchor knot.

Simple Leaf

1. Cut 1 length of ribbon 2RW. Fold the ribbon length in half, right side in, matching the raw edges. Anchor knot the thread into the selvage edges at the fold. Assembly stitch the selvage edges together; anchor knot.

2. Open the leaf and gently poke the tip out with a stuffing tool. Gather stitch across and ⅛" (3mm) above the 2 edges. Pull the thread to gather the stitches; anchor knot.

Zipper Leaf

1. Begin with 1 half of a zipper. Cut the length to 4"–6" (10.2–15.2cm).

2. Fold the length in half. Anchor knot through the selvage edges at the fold.

3. Whipstitch the edges together; anchor knot.

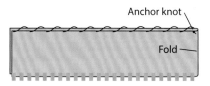

Stash Idea Inspiration

Cut a doily in half and use it as a vase, with additional trims stitched onto the base.

Fill the vase with flowers and embellish with buttons, charms, and notions. See rosette (page 54), fuller flowers (page 55), crinkly flowers (page 55), posy (page 54), rickrack flower (page 57), rickrack rose (page 58), zipper rose (page 59), simple rose (page 58).

Note: *The lace daisies were made with a Daisy Maker (below).*

Notions of Spring, 15″ × 15″ (38.1 × 38.1cm)

VINTAGE AND NEW TOOLS

A. Daisy Maker is a vintage tool that creates flowers made from yarn.

B. Ribbon Rose tool is a vintage instrument that creates a folded rose.

C. Yo-yo makers: These are new tools made by Clover MFG. Co. LTD., which helps you to make round and heart-shaped yo-yos.

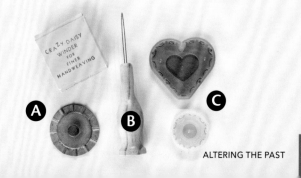

Decorative Trims

Braided Ribbon or Cord

Use narrow ribbon or cord

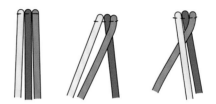

1. Work with 3 equal lengths of ribbon, cord, or other trim. Tackstitch them together at one end; anchor knot and cut the thread.

2. Alternating between the left and right lengths, wrap over the center length, tightening the braid after each wrap.

3. Cut the ends even at the desired length. Tackstitch together; anchor knot and cut the thread.

Note: *When using a wider ribbon, fold the lengths over rather than wrapping.*

Braided Rickrack

1. Work with 2 equal lengths of the same size rickrack trim.

2. Match a wave to an open section as shown and tackstitch the ends together; knot and cut the thread.

3. Interlace the length of trim together. Cut the desired length. Tackstitch the ends together; anchor knot, and cut the thread.

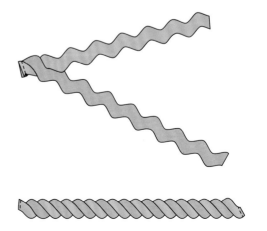

Detailed Rickrack

1. Work with 2 equal lengths of 2 different sizes of rickrack trim. Tackstitch the tails at 1 end together; anchor knot, and cut the thread.

2. Interlace the length of trim together. Cut the desired length. Tackstitch the tails together; anchor knot, and cut the thread.

Note: *A narrow ribbon can be substituted for the narrower rickrack trim.*

Knotted Ribbon

Begin ½" (1.2cm) in from one end. Tie a knot every 1" (2.5cm) measuring the desired length as you go. Cut ½" (1.2cm) from the last knot.

Fold-and-Turn Trim

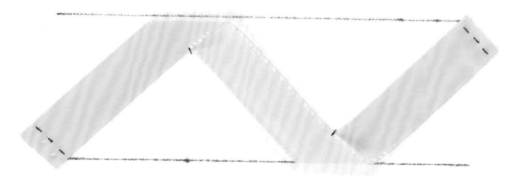

1. Draw 2 lines on the fabric base with an air-erasable pen. Thread a needle with sewing thread. Place the ribbon at an angle, with the raw edge at the bottom line; tackstitch in place.

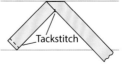

2. Fold the ribbon down and to the right, with the fold on the top line; tackstitch.

3. Repeat Step 2, folding the ribbon up and to the right.

4. Repeat Steps 2–3 to finish the row. To end the row, cut off the excess ribbon and tackstitch in place; knot and cut the thread.

Stash Idea Inspiration

Randomly patch-piece a group of upholstery fabrics and adorn the seams with trims using the techniques in this chapter. Embroider using the ideas in Stitching Creatively (page 89), embellish with little stitched extras, and vintage buttons. See braided ribbon or cord (page 62), braided rickrack (page 62), detailed rickrack (page 63), fold-and-turn trim (page 63), penny circles (page 68), fabric yo-yos (page 66), and fabric circle variations (page 68).

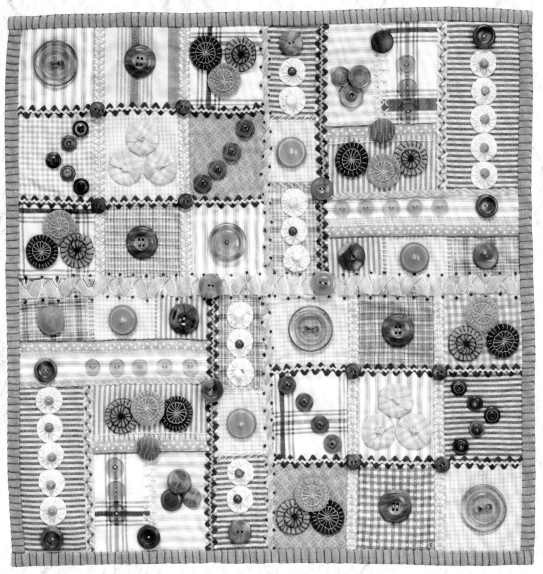

Patched and Buttoned, 20″ × 20″ (50.8 × 50.8cm)

Little Stitched Extras

Tatty Lace Bird's Nest

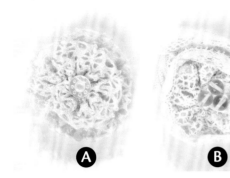

1. Cut a 12RW length of ribbon.

   A. Follow the directions for the ribbon layered with lace (page 53) with 2 or more widths of lace.

   B. Collage piece the ribbon base with overlapped short lengths of lace.

2. Follow Steps 2–5 for the rolled rose (page 59).

3. Stitch a button or beads in the center.

Woven Bird's Nest

1. Cut a 1¾″ (4.4cm) circle from crinoline. Follow Step 1 of the vintage favorite (page 56) from *, stitching 9 spokes.

2. Cut 1 yard (1m) of ½″ (1.2cm) rayon hem tape. Tackstitch the raw edge onto the center of the circle with sewing thread.

3. Follow Step 3 of the vintage favorite to ⅛″ (3mm) from the outer edge of the crinoline.

4. Cut off the excess tape 1″ (2.5cm) from the raw edge. Tackstitch the raw edge to the wrong side of the circle.

5. Turn under the remaining edge of the circle to the wrong side; whipstitch in place with perle cotton.

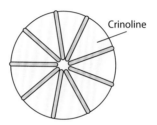

Crinoline

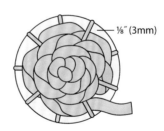

⅛″ (3mm)

Fabric Circle

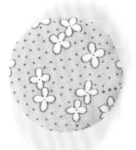

1. Cut a 1⅜" (3.5cm) circle from fast2fuse and a 1¼" (3.2cm) circle from batting. Glue the batting to the fast2fuse.

2. Cut a 2⅛" (5.4cm) circle from fabric.

3. Stitch a basting stitch ⅛" (3mm) from the raw edge of the fabric, ending with the needle on the wrong side.

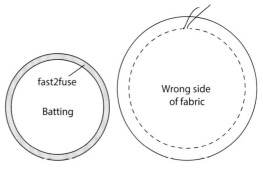

4. Place the batting side of the fast2fuse circle in the center of the wrong side of the fabric. Pull the thread to gather the stitches; anchor knot.

Note: You can use a larger or smaller circle of fast2fuse. Cut the batting ⅛" (3mm) smaller, and the fabric ¾" (1.9cm) larger.

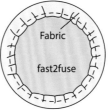

Fabric Yo-yos

1. Cut a 2" (5.1cm) circle from fabric. *Working with the wrong side of the fabric facing up, fold over a ⅛" (3mm) seam, insert the needle under the seam, and into the fold.

2. Gather stitch close to the folded edge through both layers of fabric. End the stitching on the wrong side of the fabric.

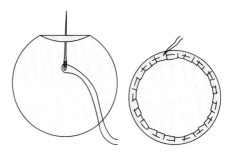

3. Pull the thread to gather the stitches and anchor knot the thread into a fold of the fabric. Bury the needle through the fold of the fabric; knot and cut the thread.

Note: You can use a larger circle.

Crazy Yo-yos

1. Hand stitch 2 or more pieces of fabric together, slightly larger than 2¼" (5.7cm).

2. Cut out 1 circle of fabric 2¼" (5.7cm). Follow the directions for the fabric yo-yos (page 66) from *.

Fabric Flower

1. From fabric, cut 5 circles 2" (5.1cm) in diameter.

2. Fold 1 circle in half, wrong side in. Anchor knot the thread on 1 edge close to the fold. Gather stitch ⅛" (3mm) from the edges and through both layers of fabric. Pull the thread to gather the stitches, anchor knot, and cut the thread.

3. Repeat Step 2 for each remaining circle.

4. Stitch through the raw edges of each petal, coming back through the first petal. Pull the thread to form the center of the flower.

5. To finish, stitch a button or yo-yo in the center of the flower.

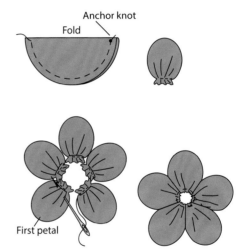

Anchor knot

Fold

First petal

Fabric Circle Variations

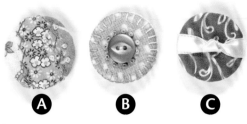

Follow the directions for the fabric circle (page 66).

A. Hand stitch 2 or more pieces of fabric together, slightly larger than 2⅛" (5.4cm).

Option: *Add embroidery stitches to the fabric seams.*

B. Stitch a button into the center. Stitch the blanket stitch (page 76) around the outer edge.

C. Cut 1 piece of ribbon 4" (10.2cm), and tie a knot in the center. Place the ribbon over the front, tackstitch the overlapped raw edges on the back.

Penny Circles

1. Cut 2 circles 1¼" (3.2cm) from felt. Cut 1 circle ⅞" (2.2cm) from a second color of felt.

Note: *Any size circle can be used, with the second size at least ⅜" (1cm) smaller.*

2. Glue the smaller circle to the center of one large circle with a fabric glue stick.

3. With perle cotton, stitch a buttonhole circle (page 81) around the outer edge of the smaller circle.

4. Place the remaining large circle under the first circle. Stitch the 2 circles together with the blanket stitch (page 76).

Options: *In Step 2, work a 3-wrap French knot stitch (page 71) into the center of the circle. In Step 4 insert a small amount of stuffing before the edges are closed to create a firmer base.*

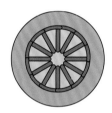

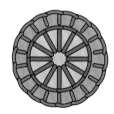

Stash Idea Inspiration

Hand stitch a doily to a solid or pieced fabric base layered with lace, ribbons, and trims. Embroider and embellish with threads, beads, buttons, and ribbonwork flowers and leaves from this chapter. See Framed Lace Collar (page 128) for ideas.

Faded Shades of Rococo Days, 14″ × 14″ (35.6 × 35.6cm)

Embroidery and Embellishment Stitches

EMBROIDERY STITCHES

The stitches listed in this section can be stitched with a variety of threads, silk embroidery ribbons, beads, sequins, buttons, and sewing notions. See Hand-Stitching Tools (page 142), Which Needle (page 142), and Embroidery and Embellishment Basics (page 143).

Note: *Use an air-erasable pen to draw in any lines, shapes, or templates.*

American Kitsch, 16″ × 19″ (40.6 × 48.3cm)

A Note from the Author

It is always a good idea to practice or refamiliarize yourself with a stitch before you work on a project. Keep a ball of perle cotton and a needle on hand with a piece of cotton muslin backed with light-weight interfacing.

Straight Stitch

Come up at **A** and go down at **B**. This stitch can be worked vertically or horizontally.

Seed Stitch

Stitch 2 straight stitches close together. Repeat, randomly filling in the section or space.

Pistil Stitch

1. Come up at **A**. Holding the needle a short distance away and close to the fabric, wrap the thread 1–3 times over the needle.

2. Go down at **B**. Pull the thread tight around the needle. Pull the needle through the fabric.

French Knot Stitch

1. Come up at **A**. Holding the needle close to the fabric, wrap the thread around the needle 1–5 times.

2. Pull the thread tight; hold the end of the thread tail with your thumb. Go down at **B**. Pull the needle and thread through the fabric.

Stamen Stitch

1. Come up at **A**. In one motion, go down at **B** and up at **C**; wrap the working thread over the needle, and under the tip.

2. Pull the needle through the fabric. To finish the stitch, go down at **D**.

Whip-Stitch Star

1. Work 3 straight stitches (above). Stitch a short stitch across the center of the stitches.

2. Come up at **A**. Go under spokes 6 and 2. Whip the thread over spoke 2, then under spokes 2 and 4. Pull the thread close to the center.

3. Continue whipping the thread over a spoke, then under the same spoke and the next spoke. To end the stitch, go down at **B** after the last spoke is covered.

Cross Stitch

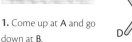

1. Come up at **A** and go down at **B**.

2. Come up at **C** and go down at **D** crossing over the first stitch.

Cross Stitch Twisted

1. Come up at **A** and go down at **B**.

2. Come up at **C**. Thread the needle under then over the previous stitch; go down at **D**, working from right to left.

Lazy Daisy Stitch

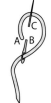

1. Come up at **A**. In one motion, go down at **B** and up at **C**. Wrap the working thread under the tip of the needle. Pull the needle through the fabric.

2. To end the stitch, go down at **D** or a short distance away for a long arm stitch.

Lazy Daisy with French Knot Stitch

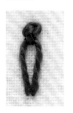

1. Follow Step 1 of the lazy daisy stitch (above).

2. Holding the needle close to the fabric, wrap the thread 1–3 times over the needle. Go down at **D**. Pull the needle through the wrapped stitches and fabric.

Lazy Daisy with Bullion Tip Stitch

1. Come up at **A**. In one motion, go down at **B** and up at **C**, but do not pull the thread through the fabric. Wrap the thread around the needle 2 or 3 times.

2. Pull the needle through the fabric. To end the stitch, go down at **D** just beyond the wraps.

Looped Tendril Stitch

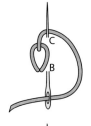
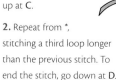

1. Follow Step 1 of the lazy daisy stitch (above). *In one motion, go down at **B** (outside of, and longer than the previous stitch) and up at **C**.

2. Repeat from *, stitching a third loop longer than the previous stitch. To end the stitch, go down at **D**.

Fly Stitch

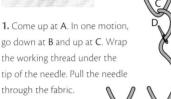

1. Come up at **A**. In one motion, go down at **B** and up at **C**. Wrap the working thread under the tip of the needle. Pull the needle through the fabric.

2. To end the stitch, go down at **D**, or a short distance away for a long tail.

Fly Stitch Offset

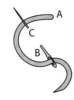

1. Come up at **A**. In one motion, go down at **B** and up at **C**. Wrap the working thread under the tip of the needle. Pull the needle through the fabric.

2. To end the stitch, go down at **D**.

Fly Stitch with French Knot Stitch

1. Follow Step 1 of the fly stitch (left). Point **C** now becomes point **A**.

2. Follow the directions for the French knot stitch (page 71) wrap 1–3 times. Go down at **D**.

Fly Stitch with Lazy Daisy Stitch

1. Follow Step 1 of the fly stitch (above). In one motion, go down at **D** and up at **E**. Wrap the working thread under the tip of the needle. Pull the needle through the fabric.

2. To end the stitch, go down at **F**.

Fleet Stitch

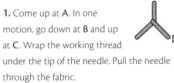

1. Come up at **A**. In one motion, go down at **B** and up at **C**. Wrap the working thread under the tip of the needle. Pull the needle through the fabric.

2. To end the stitch, go down at **D**.

Fleet Stitch with Loose Knot Stitch

1. Follow Step 1 of the fleet stitch (left). Go under the base stitch only; wrap the working thread under the tip of the needle. Pull the thread firmly around the base stitch.

2. To end the stitch, go down at **D**.

Backstitch

1. Come up at **A**. *Backstitch the needle in one motion, down at **B**, and up at **C**. Pull the needle through the fabric. Point **C** now becomes **A**.

2. Repeat from * to finish the row. To end the stitch, go down at **B**.

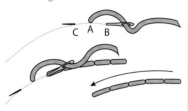

Stem Stitch

1. Come up at **A**, with the thread below the line. *Backstitch the needle in one motion down at **B** and up at **C**. Pull the needle through the fabric.

2. Repeat from * to finish the row, with **C** of the next stitch next to **B** of the previous stitch. To end the stitch, go down at **B**.

Couched Stitch

1. Stitch a length of thread onto the fabric; knot and cut the end.

2. With a different color or type of thread come up next to one end of the thread. Work straight stitches (page 71) across the row.

Note: *A heavier thread or ribbon can be used in Step 1.*

Coral Stitch

1. Come up at **A**, hold the working thread straight. *In one motion, go down at **B** and up at **C** slightly angled. Wrap the working thread under the tip of the needle.

2. Pull the needle through the fabric to form a knot.

3. Repeat from * to finish the row. To end the stitch, go down at **D** a slight distance away from the last knot.

Snail Trail Stitch

1. Come up at **A**. *In one motion, go down at **B** and up at **C**.

2. Wrap the working thread over the needle and under the tip. Place your thumb over the loop and pull the needle through the fabric.

3. Repeat from * to finish the row, a short distance away from the previous stitch. To end the stitch, go down at **D**.

Bead Strand Stitch Single

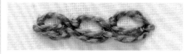

1. Come up at **A**, with the thread below the line. *In one motion, go down at **B** and up at **C**. Wrap the working thread under the eye and the tip of the needle.

2. Place your thumb over the loop and pull the needle through the fabric. Go down at **D**. Come up at **E**.

3. Repeat from * to finish the row. To end the stitch, go down at **F**.

Chain Stitch

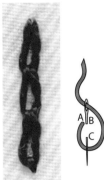

1. Come up at **A**. *In one motion, go down at **B** and up at **C**. Wrap the working thread under the tip of the needle. Pull the needle through the fabric.

2. Repeat from * to finish the row, starting inside the previous loop. To finish the stitch, go down at **D**.

Chain Stitch Spiny

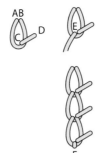

1. Come up at **A**. Follow Step 1 of the chain stitch (left) from *. Go down at **D**, angling up. Come up at **E**, which now becomes point **A** of the chain stitch.

2. Repeat from * to finish the row, working a spine outside of each chain. To end the stitch, go down at **F**.

Chain Stitch Double

1. *Follow the directions for the chain stitch (left), working the stitch slightly angled and next to the seam.

2. In one motion, go down at **D** next to **B** and up at **E** on the seam.

3. To finish the row repeat from *, beginning in the loop of the previous stitch. To end the stitch, go down at **F**.

Chain Stitch Zigzag

Follow the directions for the chain stitch (above), angling the first stitch away from the seam and the next stitch toward the seam. Repeat the pattern across the row.

Fishhook Stitch

1. Work 1 fly stitch (page 73) with point **B** higher than point **A**.

2. Repeat Step 1, working inside the previous stitch, and below, with point **A** higher than point **B**, and even with point **A** of the previous stitch.

3. To finish the row, repeat Steps 1 and 2, working the next group of stitches below the previous group.

Fly Stitch Fancy Link

1. Follow Step 1 of the fishhook stitch (left). Work a second stitch crossed over the first, with point **A** above point **B**.

2. Work 1 fly stitch with **A** and **B** worked into the 2 stitches above it, and **C** below. Wrap the working thread over the needle, and under the tip. Pull the needle through the fabric.

3. To end the stitch, go down at **D**. To finish the row, repeat Steps 1 and 2, above. End the row with either stitch.

Blanket Stitch

1. Come up at **A**. *In one motion, go down at **B** and up at **C**. Wrap the working thread under the tip of the needle. Pull the needle through the fabric.

2. Repeat from * to finish the row. To end the stitch, go down at **D**, or a short distance away.

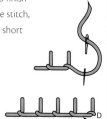

Blanket Stitch Up and Down

1. *Work 1 blanket stitch (left). In one motion, go down at **D** and up at **E**. Loop the working thread over the tip of the needle.

2. Pull the needle through the fabric. Thread the needle under the loop and gently pull the thread to tighten.

3. Repeat from * to finish the row. To end the stitch, go down at **F**.

Blanket Stitch Closed

1. Follow Step 1 of the blanket stitch (left) *with the stitch angled right to left.

2. Work a second stitch going down at **B** and up at **D** with the stitch angled left to right.

3. To finish the row, repeat from *. To end the stitch, go down at **E**.

Blanket and Chain Stitches

1. Work 1 blanket stitch (above). Work 1 chain stitch (page 75) going down at **D** and up at **E**.

2. Repeat Step 1 to finish the row. To end the stitch, go down at **F** after a blanket stitch or chain stitch.

Shell Stitch

1. Draw or follow a quarter circle. Follow Step 1 of the blanket stitch (above), with points **A** and **C** on the curved line.

2. Work a second stitch and a third stitch along the curved line. To end the stitch, go down at **D**.

Shell Stitch Row

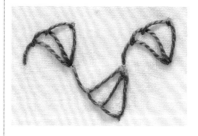

1. Work 1 shell stitch (left).

2. Work a second stitch upside down and to the right with point **A** of the new stitch close to point **B** of the previous stitch.

3. Repeat Steps 1 and 2 to finish the row.

Feather Stitch

1. Come up at **A**. *In one motion, go down at **B** and up at **C**. Wrap the working thread under the tip of the needle. Pull the needle through the fabric.

2. Repeat from * working the next stitch below and in the opposite direction.

3. Repeat Steps 1 and 2 to finish the row. To end the stitch, go down at **D**.

Feather Stitch Single

Draw a line or follow a seam.

1. Come up at **A**. Follow Step 1 of the feather stitch (left) from *, with **B** directly across from **A**, and **A** and **C** on the line.

2. Repeat from * to finish the row. To end the stitch, go down at **D**.

Feather Stitch Looped

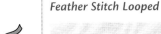

1. Come up at **A**. *In one motion, go down at **B** and up at **C**. Wrap the working thread under the eye and the tip of the needle and back to the base of the stitch. Pull the needle through the fabric. Go down at **D**, to catch the loop. Come up at **E**.

2. Repeat Step 1 from *, working the next stitch below and in the opposite direction. To end the stitch, go down at **F**.

Feather Stitch Cobwebbed

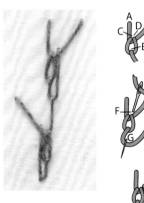

1. Follow Step 1 of the feather stitch single (above). *Work a chain stitch (page 75) from **D** to **E** inside the loop, and on the line. Work a second chain stitch from **F** to **G**, wider and below the first.

2. Work a second stitch below, and in the opposite direction. Follow Step 1 from *.

3. Repeat Steps 1 and 2 above to finish the row. To end the stitch, go down at **H**.

Feather Stitch Double

1. Follow Step 1 of the feather stitch (above). Work a second stitch below and in the same direction.

2. Follow Step 2 of the feather stitch. Work a second stitch below and in the same direction.

3. Repeat Steps 1 and 2 above to finish the row. To end the stitch, go down at **D**.

Fern Stitch Modern

Draw a line or follow a seam.

1. Work a straight stitch (page 71) on the line. *Work 1 fly stitch with a long tail (page 73); the tail is the beginning of the next stitch. **Note:** A and B are even with the top of the straight stitch and C and D are the same length as the straight stitch.

2. Repeat from * to finish the row.

Cretan Stitch

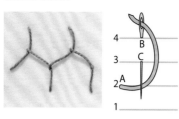

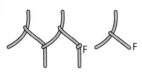

Work this stitch between 4 horizontal rows.

1. Come up at **A** on line 2. *In one motion, go down at **B** on line 4 and up at **C** on line 3. Wrap the working thread under the tip of the needle. Pull the needle through the fabric.

2. In one motion, go down at **D** on line 1 and up at **E** on line 2. Wrap the working thread under the tip of the needle. Pull the needle through the fabric.

3. Repeat from * to finish the row. To end the stitch, go down at **F**, either after Step 1 or Step 2.

Cretan Stitch Up and Down

1. Follow Step 1 of the cretan stitch (left). *In one motion, go down at **F** and up at **G**. Loop the working thread over the tip of the needle. Pull the needle through the fabric. Pass the needle under the loop and gently pull the thread to tighten.

2. Follow Step 2 of the cretan stitch, repeat Step 1 from *.

3. Repeat Steps 1 and 2 above to finish the row. To end the stitch, go down **H**.

Cretan Stitch with Chain Stitch

1. Follow Step 1 of the cretan stitch (above). *In one motion, go down at **F** and up at **G**. Wrap the working thread under the tip of the needle. Pull the needle through the fabric.

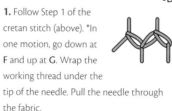

2. Follow Step 2 of the cretan stitch and Step 1 above from *.

3. Repeat Steps 1 and 2 above to finish the row. To end the stitch, go down at **H**.

Cretan Stitch with Feather Stitch

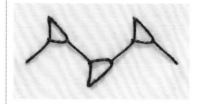

1. Follow Step 1 of the cretan stitch (left). *In one motion, go down at **F** and up at **G**. Wrap the working thread under the tip of the needle. Pull the needle through the fabric.

2. Follow Step 2 of the cretan stitch and Step 1 above from *.

3. Repeat Steps 1 and 2 above to finish the row. To end the stitch, go down at **H**.

Cretan Stitch Looped

1. Come up at **A**. *In one motion, go down at **B** and up at **C**. Wrap the working thread under the eye and the tip of the needle and back to the base of the stitch. Pull the needle through the fabric. Go down at **D**.

2. Come up at **E**. In one motion, go down at **F** and up at **G**. Follow Step 1 from *, going down at **H**.

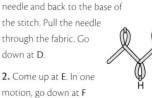

3. Repeat Steps 1 from * and 2 to finish the row. To end the stitch, go down at **I**.

Crossed Wing Stitch

1. Come up at **A** and go down at **B**.

2. Come up at **C**. Cross over the previous stitch then under the stitch and up. Cross over this new stitch, then go down at **D**.

3. To finish the row repeat Steps 1 and 2, with **A**, crossing over the stitch in Step 2.

Cross Stitch Row

1. Come up at **A** go down at **B**. Repeat this step across the row.

2. Come up at **C** and go down at **D**. Repeat this step across the row.

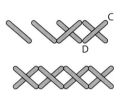

Herringbone Stitch

Work this stitch between 2 horizontal rows.

1. Come up at **A**. *Backstitch the needle in one motion down at **B** and up at **C**. Pull the needle through the fabric. Repeat from *, going down at **D** and up at **A**.

2. Repeat Step 1 to finish the row. To end the stitch, go down at **B** or **D**.

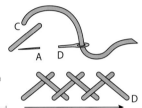

Herringbone Stitch Twisted

1. Come up at **A** and go down at **B**.

2. Come up at **C**. Thread the needle under then over the previous stitch, go down at **D**.

3. Repeat Steps 1 and 2 to finish the row. To end the stitch, go down at **D**.

Chevron Stitch

Work this stitch between 2 horizontal rows.

1. Come up at **A**. Backstitch in one motion down at **B** up at **C**. Pull the needle through the fabric.

2. Backstitch in one motion down at **D** and up at **E**. Pull the needle through the fabric. Backstitch in one motion down at **F** and up at **D**.

3. Repeat Step 2 to finish the row, alternating the stitches between the lines. To end the stitch, go down at **F**.

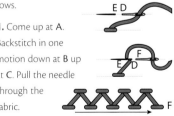
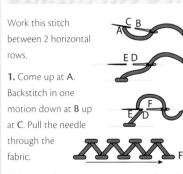

Flower Templates

Choose a template and draw in the lines for the straight stitch, lazy daisy, or fly stitch flowers.

Work the petals in the order they are shown.

Option: *Work a French knot (page 71) in the center of the flower.*

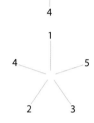

Straight Stitch Flowers

Suggested stitches: Straight stitch (page 71), pistil stitch (page 71), or stamen stitch (page 71).

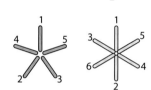

Lazy Daisy Stitch Flowers

Suggested stitches: Lazy daisy stitch (page 72), lazy daisy with French knot stitch (page 72), or lazy daisy with bullion tip stitch (page 72).

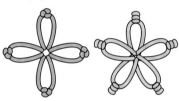

Fly Stitch Flowers

Note: *The lines for the petals represents the center of the stitch.*

Suggested stitches: Fly stitch (page 73) or fly stitch with French knot stitch (page 71).

French Knot Stitch Flowers

1. Work a 3-wrap French Knot stitch (page 71) for the center.

2. With the same thread or a different color, work 4 to 6 French knot stitches, 2 wraps each, around the center in the order as shown, stitching close to the center or further away.

Spiderweb Rose Stitch and Variation

Variation: *Work with a blend of 2 or more colors of threads. See Note below.*

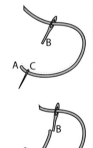

1. Draw a circle, then draw 5 equally-spaced spokes. Work straight stitches (page 71) from the outer edge of the circle to the center. Knot and cut the thread.

2. Thread a chenille needle with 30″ (76.2cm) of the same or heavier weight thread. Come up at **A**.

3. Weave the needle and thread over and under the spokes counterclockwise, pulling the thread through the spokes. To end the stitch, go down at **B**.

Note: *When working with a blend of threads, twirl the needle to the right to twist the threads.*

Whip-Stitch Rose and Variation

Variation: *Work with a blend of 2 or more colors of threads. See Note above.*

1. Draw a circle with a smaller circle in the center. Work straight stitches (page 71) from the outer circle to the inner circle. Knot and cut the thread.

2. Thread a chenille needle with the same or heavier weight thread. Come up at **A**.

3. Working clockwise, thread the needle over the spoke, and backstitch under the next 2 spokes. Gently pull the thread to whip around the spoke.

4. Repeat Step 3, working around the spokes to the outer edges. To end, wrap the thread over the previous spoke, and go down at **B**.

5. Fill the center with French knot stitches (page 71).

Bell Flower Stitch

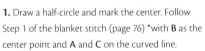

1. Draw a half-circle and mark the center. Follow Step 1 of the blanket stitch (page 76) *with **B** as the center point and **A** and **C** on the curved line.

2. Repeat from *, working the stitches around the curve. To end the stitch, go down at **D**.

Buttonhole Circle Stitch

1. Draw a circle and mark the center point. Follow Step 1 of the blanket stitch (page 76) *with point **B** as the center of the stitch and points **A** and **C** on the curved line.

2. Repeat from *, working the stitches around the circle. To end the stitch, go down next to the first stitch.

Padded Straight Stitch

1. Work 1 straight stitch (page 71).

2. Work a second stitch over and slightly longer than the first.

Pointed Petal Stitch

1. Come up at **A** and go down at **B**. Pull the ribbon through the fabric to form a point at the tip. Set the needle aside.

2. Thread a needle with sewing thread. Come up at **C** through the ribbon; go down at **D** at the tip of the ribbon. Knot and cut both the thread and ribbon.

Ruched Rose Stitch

1. Come up through the fabric. Hold the needle a short distance away from the fabric. Wrap the ribbon around the needle 2–3 times.

2. Gather stitch the needle down through the length of the ribbon.

3. Stitch through the end of the ribbon and the fabric, pulling the ribbon gently to form the petals.

Heartful Stitch

1. Draw the dots. Come up at **A**. Twirl the needle to the right to twist the ribbon.

2. Going down at **B** then up at **C**, pull the needle through the fabric, catching the loop of ribbon. Go down at **D**.

3. Work a second stitch angled to the left, twirling the needle to the left to twist the ribbon, stitching into points **A** and **B** of the first stitch.

Woven Rose Stitch

1. Thread a needle with perle cotton and follow Step 1 for the spiderweb rose stitch (page 81).

2. Thread a needle with silk embroidery ribbon. Come up at **A**, *twist the ribbon slightly to the right.

3. Weave the needle and thread over and under the spokes counterclockwise, pulling the ribbon through the spokes. To end the stitch, go down at **B**.

Note: *Two different colors and/or sizes of ribbon can be used.*

Woven Rose Stitch Variation

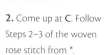

1. Follow Steps 1–3 of the woven rose stitch (left) to create a center. Go down at **B**.

2. Come up at **C**. Follow Steps 2–3 of the woven rose stitch from *.

Note: *Two different colors and/or sizes of ribbon can be used.*

Ribbon Loop Stitch

 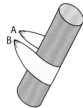

1. Come up at **A** and go down at **B**.

2. Insert a porcupine quill or straw into the center of the loop. Pull the ribbon through the fabric to the desired length.

Silk Ribbon Flower Stitch

1. Draw the short lines of the flower.

2. Work the petals with the ribbon loop stitch (left).

Option: *Work a French knot stitch into the center.*

Ribbon Stitch

1. Come up at **A**. Hold the ribbon flat against the fabric. Go down at **B** through the ribbon.

2. Form a curved tip by gently pulling the ribbon through the stitch.

French Knot Bud Stitch

1. Come up at **A**. Twirl the needle to the right to twist the ribbon. Wrap the ribbon around the needle loosely 5 times.

2. Go down close to **A**, arranging the wraps down the needle and against the fabric, with the last wrap forming the outer ring and the first wrap as the center.

3. Pull the needle through the fabric. Knot the thread.

4. Tackstitch around the outer ring with sewing thread.

English Rose Stitch

1. Stitch 5 loose French knot stitches (page 71) with 3–5 wraps.

2. Come up at **A**. Working counterclockwise, stitch the stem stitch (page 74) around the center knots.

3. Work one row around the center and go down after the last stitch.

Note: *Two different sizes and/or colors of ribbon can be used.*

Ellen Matilda's Rose Stitch

1. Follow Steps 1–3 of the woven rose stitch (page 82).

2. Come up at **C**. Work 1 row of chain stitches (page 75) around the center. To end the stitch, go down at **D**.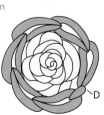

Note: *Two different colors and/ or sizes of ribbon can be used.*

GENERAL RIBBONWORK DIRECTIONS

1. Cut a length of ribbon using the ribbon measurement guide.

2. Thread a small sharps needle with thread.

3. Come up through the fabric. Follow the directions for the flower.

RIBBON MEASUREMENT GUIDE

Flower	Silk embroidery ribbon		
	4mm	7mm	13mm
Rosette Stitch	2" (5.1cm)	3" (7.6cm)	5" (12.7cm)
Posy Stitch	2" (5.1cm)	3" (7.6cm)	5" (12.7cm)
Old Rose Stitch	4" (10.2cm)	6" (15.2cm)	8" (20.3cm)

Rosette Stitch

1. Stitch through the ribbon ⅛" (3mm), from the raw and inner selvage edges.

2. Gather stitch along the inner selvage edge, stopping ¼" (6mm) from the opposite raw edge, and fold the edge under. The needle should be on the wrong side of the ribbon.

3. Go down through the ribbon and fabric close to the beginning stitch. Pull the thread to create the center of the flower. Knot the thread. Tackstitch the center and outer edges of the flower.

Posy Stitch

1. Stitch through the ribbon ⅛" (3mm), from the raw and top selvage edges.

2. Gather stitch at an angle down to the inner selvage edge and continue along the bottom edge to ⅛" (3mm) from the selvage edge. Stop and angle to the top selvage and raw edges.

3. Go down through the ribbon close to the beginning of the stitch and through the fabric. Pull the thread to create the center of the flower. Knot the thread. Tackstitch the center and outer edges of the flower.

Old Rose Stitch

1. Fold the length of ribbon in half. Follow Steps 1 and 2 of the posy stitch (above), beginning at the raw edges and stitching through both layers of ribbon.

2. Pull the thread to create the flower. Wrap the ribbon around the center; go down through the fabric at the edge of the rose.

Single Bead Stitch

1. Come up and thread 1 bead onto the needle. Lay the bead flat against the fabric. Go down beyond the edge of the bead.

2. Come up and pass the needle through the bead a second time and down. Knot the thread after every 4 stitches.

Grouped Bead Stitch

Follow the directions for the single bead stitch (left), but with 2 or 3 beads of the same size. Knot the thread after every 2 stitches.

Bead Combination Stitch

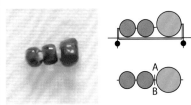

1. Follow the directions for the single bead stitch (left), but with a group of different sizes and shapes of beads.

2. Come up at **A** between the large and small beads and go down at **B** to couch the thread. Knot the thread after every 2 stitches.

Stacked Bead Stitch

Base bead: Come up and thread 1 large bead onto the needle, placing the bead against the fabric.

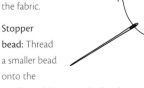

Stopper bead: Thread a smaller bead onto the needle. Holding onto the bead, pass the needle back through the base bead and down. Knot the thread.

Bead Cascade Stitch

Base bead: Come up and thread 1 large bead onto the needle, placing the bead against the fabric.

Cascade: Thread 3–7 or more smaller beads onto the needle and go down just beyond the edge of the larger bead. Knot the thread.

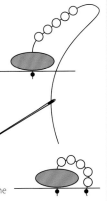

Continuous Bead Stitch

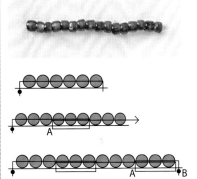

1. Come up and *thread 6 beads onto the needle; lay the beads flat against the fabric. Go down just beyond the edge of the last bead.

2. Come up at **A**, between the third and fourth bead in the row. Thread the needle through the remaining beads in the row. To finish the row, continue from *.

3. To end the stitch come up at **A**. Go down through the last 3 beads in the row and go down at **B**. Knot the thread.

Note: *For a curved row work with 4 beads, come up between the second and third beads in the row.*

Sequin Decoration Stitches

Stitch a single or group of sequins with the stitches below.

Suggested stitches: Stacked bead stitch (page 85) or bead cascade stitch (page 85)

Button Hole Decoration Stitches

Stitch the button in place with perle cotton, then follow the suggestions below.

Suggested stitches: Single bead stitch (page 85), stacked bead stitch (page 85), grouped bead stitch (page 85), or bead cascade stitch (page 85)

Snail Stitch

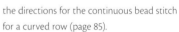

1. Draw the shape onto the fabric.

2. Stitch a single bead stitch (page 85) with a size 8° seed bead. Knot the thread.

3. Come up next to the size 8° bead, *thread 4 size 11° seed beads onto the needle. Follow the directions for the continuous bead stitch for a curved row (page 85).

4. To continue the stitch, repeat from *, wrapping the curve tightly around the size 8° bead, stitching 24–28 or more beads.

Note: *A piece of Pellon 809 Décor-Bond can be used as a base for the shape. Once the stitch is finished, trim the base close to the beads.*

Sideview Butterfly Stitch

Draw in the lines. Use silk embroidery ribbon for the body and wings, and perle cotton for the antennae.

Body: Stitch 1 padded straight stitch (page 82).

Wings: Stitch 2 lazy daisy stitches (page 72).

Antennae: Stitch 2 straight stitches (page 71).

Curved Wing Butterfly Stitch

Draw a half-circle, and mark the center.

Wings: Stitch 2 looped tendril stitches (page 72).

Body and Antennae: Stitch 2 pistil stitches (page 71) slightly angled. Couch with straight stitches (page 71).

Legs: Stitch 2 straight stitches.

BzzyBee Stitch

Draw in the lines. Use silk embroidery ribbon for the body and wings.

Body: Stitch 1 lazy daisy stitch with French knot stitch (page 71).

Wings: Stitch 4 ribbon stitches (page 83).

Stitched 2-Hole Buttons

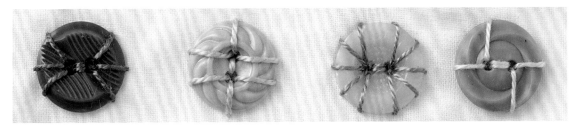

The holes of the button can be stitched in a variety of patterns, with the stitches extending beyond the edge of the button.

Stitched 4-Hole Buttons

The holes of the button can be stitched with a straight stitch in a variety of patterns.

Stacked Buttons

Stack and stitch a smaller 2- or 4-hole button on top of a larger button with the same number of holes.

Button Cascade

Stitch flat 2- or 4-hole buttons cascading down a line or curve.

Clustered Buttons

Stitch 2- or 4-hole buttons along with buttons with shanks into a group.

Embroidered Buttons

Stitch a 2- or 4-hole button in place, then add an embroidery stitch through the holes in the button or around the outer edge

Lazy daisy stitch

French knot stitch

Blanket stitch

Button Bug

Body: 1 button

Wings: Lazy daisy stitches (page 72)

Antennae and legs: Pistil stitch (page 71)

Steampunk Bugs

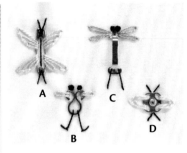

A. SAFETY-PIN BUTTERFLY

Body: 1 safety pin

Wings: Looped tendril stitch (page 72)

Antennae, legs, detail: Straight stitch (page 71)

B. HOOK GNAT

Body: 1 loop hook

Wings: Lazy daisy stitch (page 72)

Antennae and legs: French knot stitch (page 71), fly stitch offset (page 73)

C. HOOK DRAGONFLY

Body: 1 flat hook

Wings: Lazy daisy stitch (page 72)

Antennae and legs: French knot stitch (page 71), straight stitch (page 71)

D. SNAP FLY

Body: 1 snap

Wings: Fly stitch (page 73)

Antennae and legs: Straight stitch (page 71)

Spider Stitches

BUTTON SPIDER

Head and body: 1 large, 1 small button

Legs: Fly stitch offset (page 73)

BEAD SPIDER

Head and body: Single bead stitch (page 85) 1 large, 1 small

Legs: Fly stitch offset (page 73)

Spiderwebs: Corner and Round

Round

Corner

Spokes: Work each straight stitch (page 71) in the order listed.

Web: Begin at the outer edge and work long stem stitches (page 74), in rows or in a continuous stitch, back into the center of the web.

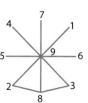

Stitching Creatively

Bella Fleur Mouchoir, 25½″ × 21½″ (64.8 × 54.6cm)

Create a base from vintage hankies combined with scraps of fabric, and ribbons. Work the embroidery stitches around the edges of the hankies and ribbons and the seams of the pieced fabric, using ideas included in this chapter. See Tea Cozy (page 121), and Flowers and Leaves (page 54) for ideas.

EMBROIDERY SKETCHBOOK

The embroidered rows and vignettes that you stitch onto your creations can be worked in the same or different weights of perle cotton or floss, or different sizes of silk embroidery ribbon. And, you can add embellishments such as buttons, beads, sequins, and charms.

In the following pages, you will find hand-illustrated embroidery designs for seams, ribbons, laces, rickrack trims, and hankies. The stitches within a design can be worked in the same colors or a variety of colors.

See Attaching Ribbon, Lace, and Trims to Fabric (page 52) for basic hand-stitching directions and Glossary of Hand-Sewn Stitches (page 52) for basic stitch terminology. See Embroidery and Embellishment Stitches (page 70) for directions and refer to the Visual Guide (page 6) for the page numbers of the embroidery stitches.

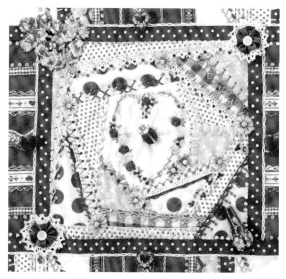

Example of seam designs, ribbon, and rickrack trim designs

Example of lace and doily edge designs

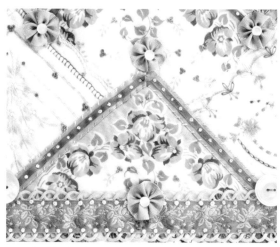

Example of hanky designs

Seams

The embroidery stitches can be worked on either side of a seam or straddling the seam.

Begin with a continuous border row stitch, then add decorative and detail stitches.

Note: *A seed bead can be used in place of a French knot stitch and vice versa.*

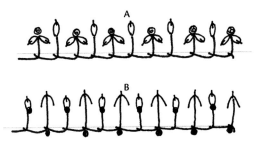

A. Blanket stitch, lazy daisy stitch, French knot stitch
B. Blanket stitch short/long, lazy daisy stitch, fly stitch,
single bead stitch

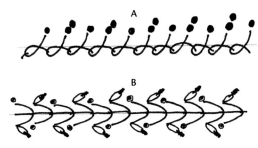

A. Snail trail stitch, single bead stitch, grouped bead stitch
B. Fern stitch modern, lazy daisy with bullion tip stitch,
French knot stitch

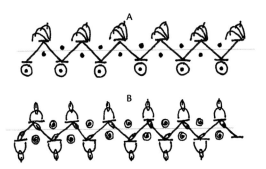

A. Chevron stitch, shell stitch, sequin decoration
stitch, single bead stitch
B. Chevron stitch, fly with lazy daisy stitch,
French knot stitch

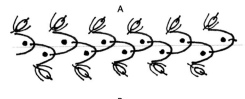

A. Feather stitch, lazy daisy stitch, fly stitch, single bead stitch
B. Feather stitch double, looped tendril stitch, pistil stitch,
French knot stitch

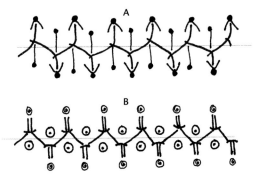

A. Cretan stitch, fly stitch with French knot stitch, pistil stitch
B. Cretan stitch up and down, stacked bead stitch,
French knot stitch

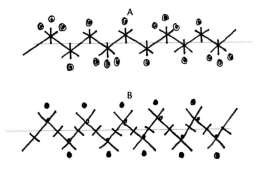

A. Herringbone stitch, straight stitch, French knot stitch
B. Herringbone stitch twisted, straight stitch, single bead stitch

Ribbon

The embroidery stitches can be worked over the edge of the ribbon, through the ribbon, or on the outer edges of the ribbon. You can also add decorative and detail stitches.

Note: *Use any consistent pattern on the ribbon, like dots, or stripes as a guide for even stitching.*

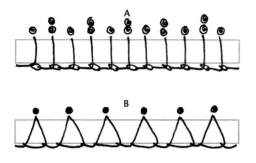

A. Blanket and chain stitches, French knot stitch
B. Blanket stitch closed, single bead stitch

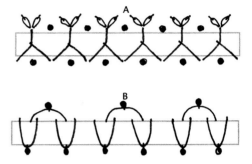

A. Fleet stitch, lazy daisy stitch, single bead stitch
B. Fly stitch with French knot stitch

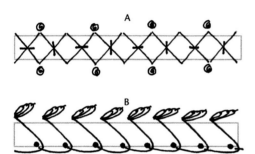

A. Cross stitch row, straight stitch, French knot stitch
B. Feather stitch single, looped tendril stitch, single bead stitch

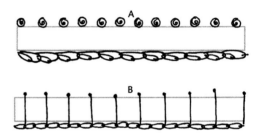

A. Chain stitch double, French knot stitch
B. Chain stitch, pistil stitch

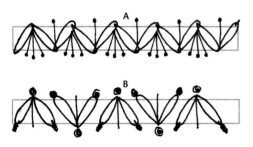

A. Chain stitch zigzag, pistil stitch
B. Lazy daisy with bullion tip stitch, lazy daisy with French knot stitch, French knot stitch, straight stitch.

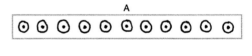

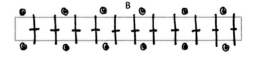

A. Stacked bead stitch
B. Straight stitch, French knot stitch

Lace

The embroidery stitches can be worked into the open areas of the lace pattern or along the outer edge of the lace.

Note: *You can stitch buttons, sequins, or stacked beads over any ripped or torn areas of the lace.*

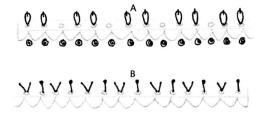

A. Lazy daisy stitch, French knot stitch
B. Straight stitch, pistil stitch

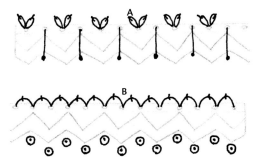

A. Lazy daisy stitch, pistil stitch
B. Fly stitch, stacked bead stitch

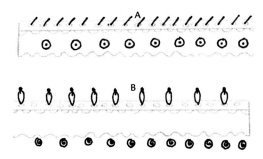

A. Straight stitch, stacked bead stitch
B. Lazy daisy with French knot stitch, French knot stitch

Rickrack

The embroidery stitches can be worked over the trim or between the curved wave edges of the trim.

Note: *Use more elaborate stitch patterns on a wide rickrack and simpler stitch patterns on a narrower one.*

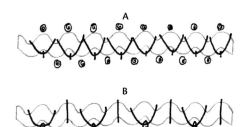

A. Fly stitch, French knot stitch
B. Fly with lazy daisy stitch, straight stitch

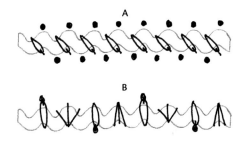

A. Lazy daisy stitch, single bead stitch
B. Lazy daisy with French knot stitch, straight stitch

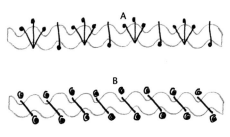

A. Pistil stitch
B. Straight stitch, French knot stitch

Hankies

The embroidery stitches can be worked around the outer edge, over the edge, or in the inside portion of the hanky.

Note: *If the hanky has a printed or an embroidered design, you can further enhance the pattern with embroidery stitches.*

Blanket stitch, lazy daisy stitch, French knot stitch

Stem stitch, lazy daisy stitch, pistil stitch, straight stitch, single bead stitch

Chain stitch, fly stitch, pistil stitch

French knot stitch

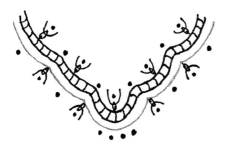

Couched stitch, fly with lazy daisy stitch, single bead stitch

Lazy daisy stitch, French knot stitch

PROJECTS BY DESIGN

WHAT CAN I DO WITH MY PILE OF STUFF?

These wallhangings showcase a variety of materials, threads, ribbons, beads, and other embellishments. Rummage through your stash and let the creativity flow! See Sewing Basics (page 141), Attaching Ribbon, Lace, and Trims to Fabric (page 52), and Glossary of Hand-Sewn Stitches (page 52).

Option: Each project has 4 sections with 2 different block designs. For a smaller project, just make 1 section, adjusting the quantities and measurements as needed.

Lace, Doilies, and Appliqués, (page 96).

A Note from the Author

If you are hesitant to use your precious treasures ask yourself this, who will see them stored away in a box? Create a Signature Label (page 113) to keep track of the components or to honor the "gift-givers" by name.

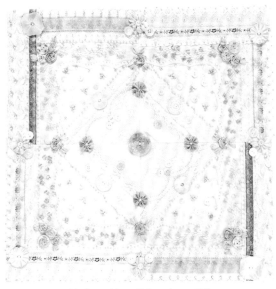

Hanky and Lace Collage (page 102)

Ribbons and Trims Squared (page 108)

Lace, Doilies, and Appliqués

Size: 14″ × 14″ (35.6 × 35.6cm)

This project starts with 2 printed fabrics, scrap fabrics, and lace for the base, with a doily and wide lace for the baskets. Floral appliqués, yo-yos, and ribbonwork flowers fill the baskets, then are embellished with embroidery stitches, beads, charms, and buttons.

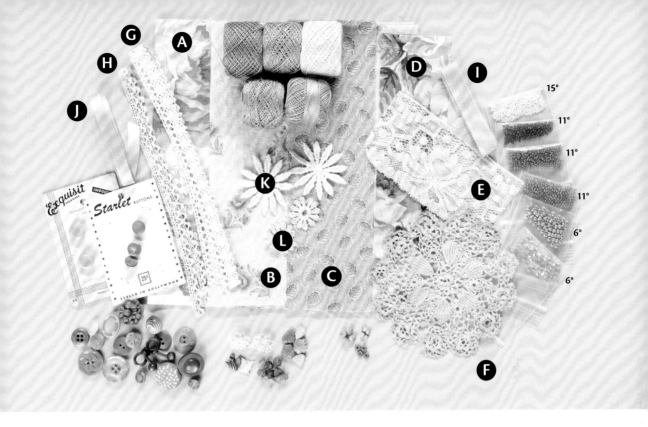

Materials

Fabric

A. ½ yard (45.7cm)

B. ¼ yard (22.9cm)

C and D. Scraps

Ribbons and trims

E. 2½″ (6.4cm) lace: ⅜ yard (34.3cm)

F. 5½″ (14cm) doily: 1 cut in half

Option: *You can use 2 different patterns of lace, or a sleeve cuff instead of a doily.*

G. ⅝″ (1.6cm) lace: 1 yard (1m)

H. ⅜″ (1cm) lace: 1½ yards (1.4m)

I. ⅝″ (1.6cm) hem tape: 10 yards (9.2m)

J. ⅜″ (1cm) satin ribbon: 2 yards (1.9m)

Perle cotton #8 and #12: 5 colors

Flower appliqués

K. 1¾″ (4.4cm): 6

L. 1″ (2.5cm): 14

Buttons: 68 in a variety of sizes and styles

Novelty-shape beads, roundels, and charms: 72 in a variety of sizes

3mm and larger glass beads: Small amounts

Seed beads (SB): Small amounts

Size 6°: 2 colors

Size 11°: 3 colors

Size 15°: 3 colors

Pellon SF 101 Shape-Flex Interfacing: ½ yard (45.7cm)

Batting: ½ yard (45.7cm)

fast2fuse Double-Sided Heavyweight Fusible: ½ yard (45.7cm)

Crinoline fabric: Small amount

Fray Check

Sewing thread

Beading thread

Wooden knitting needle or ruler for hanging

Cutting

Fabric A

- 2 squares 7¾" × 7¾" (19.7 × 19.7cm) for the base

- 1 square 14" × 14" (35.6 × 35.6cm) for the backing

- 1 rectangle 4" × 11½" (10.2 × 29.2cm) for the hanging sleeve (optional)

Fabric B

- 2 squares 7¾" × 7¾" (19.7 × 19.7cm) for the base

2½" (6.4cm) lace

- 2 lengths 5" (12.7cm) for the baskets; trim one edge on each to a slight curve.

⅝" (1.6cm) lace

- 2 lengths 15" (38.1cm) for the seamlines

Shape-Flex

- 1 square 15" × 15" (38.1 × 38.1cm)

fast2fuse

- 1 square 14" × 14" (35.6 × 35.6cm)

Batting

- 1 square 13½" × 13½" (34.3 × 34.3cm)

Hem tape

- 2 lengths 15" (38.1cm) for backing

- 2 lengths 15½" (39.4cm) for the backing

Satin ribbon

- 2 lengths 6" (15.2cm) for custom hanger

Cut a doily in half or into 4 smaller sections to create a vase or appliqué.

Note: *Place Fray Check on the cut edges of each piece of lace or doily.*

BLOCK ASSEMBLY

1. Stitch the Fabric A and B squares 7¾" × 7¾" (19.7 × 19.7cm) together with a ¼" (6mm) seam allowance to make the base.

2. Fuse the interfacing to the wrong side of the base.

3. Hand stitch the 2 pieces of ⅝" (1.6cm) lace over the seams.

4. Staystitch ¼" (6mm) from the raw edges of the base.

5. Draw temporary guidelines at ⅜" (1cm) and 1" (2.5cm) as shown.

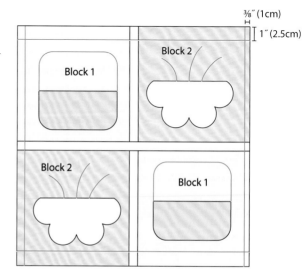

Block assembly with temporary guidelines

EMBROIDERY AND EMBELLISHMENTS

Refer to the Visual Guide (page 6) for the page numbers of the embroidery stitches. See materials for trim identification and abbreviations.

Block 1

Block 1

1. Center and hand stitch the lace basket between the seams and guidelines. Embroider the outer edge with chain stitch double.

2. By freehand, draw a handle guideline. Hand stitch 10" (25.4cm) of the ⅜" (1cm) lace on the line. Embroider with the straight stitch.

3. Hand stitch 3 large and 3 small flower appliqués in place. Embroider with the lazy daisy stitch or lazy daisy with French knot stitch.

4. Make 3 fuller flowers (page 55) from hem tape using the 12RW measurement.

5. Make 5 fabric yo-yos (page 66) from fabric C.

6. Arrange and hand stitch the flowers and yo-yos around the flower appliqués.

7. Stitch a button in the center of each large appliqué and fuller flower.

8. Stitch a flower bead in the center of each yo-yo.

9. Stitch a flower roundel and 15° SB in the center of the smaller appliqués, using the stacked bead stitch.

10. Stitch the remaining buttons, charms, and beads in place.

11. Repeat to make 2 blocks.

Block 2

Block 2

1. Center and hand stitch the doily basket between the seams and guidelines. Embroider the outer edge with the blanket stitch.

2. By freehand, draw in 3 frond guidelines. Hand stitch each line with 3″ (7.6cm) of the ⅜″ (1cm) lace. Stitch a group of 3 stacked bead stitches with 6° and 11° **SB** at the tips.

3. Embroider 4 chain stitch vines with lazy daisy stitch leaves around the fronds.

4. Make 2 vintage favorites (page 56), each using hem tape with crinoline as the base.

5. Make 5 fabric yo-yos (page 66) from fabric D.

6. Make 6 rosettes (page 54) from satin ribbon.

7. Arrange and hand stitch the flowers and yo-yos around the lace fronds.

8. Stitch a stacked bead stitch in the center of the rosettes with 6° and 11° **SB**. Stitch a stacked bead stitch in the center of the yo-yos with a larger bead and 11° **SB**.

9. Hand stitch 4 smaller appliqués in place on the tip of each chain stitch vine. Embroider with the picot stitch. Stitch a stacked bead stitch in the center with a flower roundele and 11° **SB**.

10. Stitch in the remaining buttons, charms, and beads.

11. Repeat to make 2 blocks.

FINISHING

Firm-Back Assembly

1. Press the wrong side of the backing to the fast2fuse.

2. Center and press the batting to the other side of the fast2fuse.

3. Right sides together, machine stitch 15" (38.1cm) lengths of hem tape to each vertical raw edge of the embroidered base along the staystitch line.

4. Repeat Step 3 for the 15½" (39.4cm) lengths of hem tape and the horizontal raw edges.

5. Place the embroidered base onto the batting.

6. Fold, press, and pin the hem tape to the backing on the vertical edges. Hand stitch in place.

7. Repeat Step 6 for the horizontal edges of hem tape, tucking in the ends first.

Optional: Instead of using a Custom Hanger, cut and sew a hanging sleeve (page 107) to the backing before ironing it to the fast2fuse.

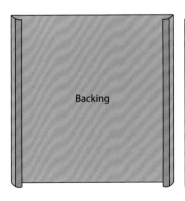
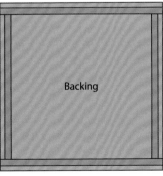

Custom Hanger

1. Cut 2 pieces of ⅜" (1cm) ribbon twice the length needed, plus ½" (1.2cm).

2. Fold the length in half, right side in. Hand stitch the raw edges together with a ¼" (6mm) seam allowance.

3. Turn the ribbon right side out. Pin the seamed end of the ribbon to the backing 1½" (3.8cm) down from the top edge and 3" (7.6cm) in from the side edges.

4. Hand stitch to the backing.

5. Insert a wooden knitting needle, ruler, or other object for the hanger.

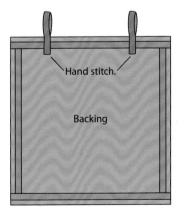

Custom hanger

Hanky and Lace Collage

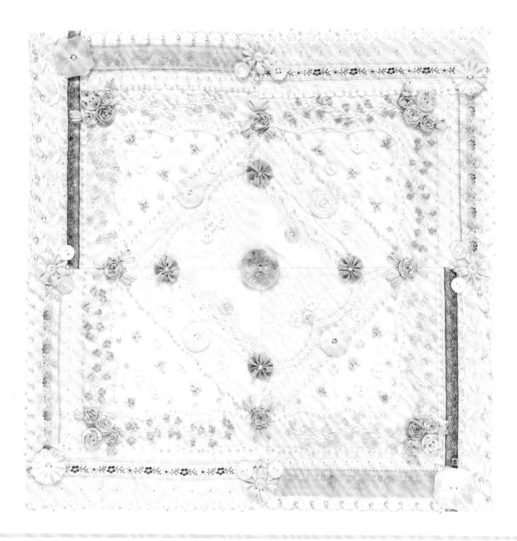

Size: 16¾" × 16¾" (42.5 × 42.5cm)

This project starts with a printed fabric, a hanky, and varying widths of vintage lace and jacquard ribbons. The collage design is embroidered with silk embroidery ribbon, silk, and rayon floss. Embellishments include rosettes, buttons, sequins, and beads.

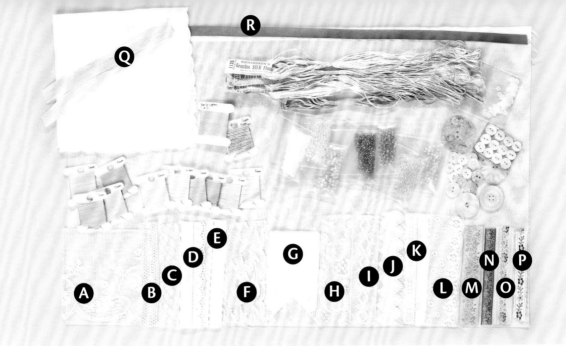

Materials

Fabric: ¾ yard (68.6cm)

Hanky 11″ × 11″ (27.9 × 27.9cm): 1 with 4 embroidered corners

Lace: ¾ yard (68.6cm) each in the following widths and types

A. 4½″ (11.4cm) edging lace

B. ⅝″ (1.6cm) insertion lace

C. ⅞″ (2.2cm) edging lace

D. 1″ (2.5cm) embroidered batiste eyelet

E. ⅝″ (1.6cm) embroidered batiste eyelet

F. 1⅝″ (4.1cm) edging lace

G. 3½″ (8.9cm) embroidered batiste eyelet

H. 1½″ (3.8cm) galloon lace

I. ⅞″ (2.2cm) insertion lace

J. 1″ (2.5cm) embroidered batiste eyelet

K. ⅞″ (2.2cm) embroidered batiste eyelet

L. 1⅜″ (3.5cm) edging lace

Ribbons: ¾ yard (68.6cm) each in the following widths and types

M. ¾″ (1.9cm) jacquard ribbon

N. ⅜″ (1cm) jacquard ribbon

O. ¾″ (1.9cm) jacquard ribbon

P. ½″ (1.2cm) jacquard ribbon

Q. ⅝″ (1.6cm) rayon hem tape

R. ⅜″ (1cm) satin ribbon

Embroidery threads: 1 spool or skein each

Perle cotton: 1 flower color

Silk, rayon, or cotton floss (SF): 5 flower colors, 1 accent color, 1 green color

Silk embroidery ribbon (SER): 1 spool or card each

2mm: 1 flower color

4mm: 5 flower colors, 1 leaf color

7mm: 3 flower colors

Seed beads (SB): small amounts

Size 6°: 3 colors

Size 11°: 3 colors

Size 15°: 1 color

Buttons: 53 in a variety of sizes and styles

Sequin: novelty or standard, 1 package

Pellon SF 101 Shape-Flex Interfacing: ½ yard (45.7cm)

Batting: ½ yard (45.7cm)

Sewing thread

Beading thread

Cutting

Fabric

- 4 squares 9″ × 9″ (22.9 × 22.9cm) for the blocks
- 1 square 17½″ × 17½″ (44.5 × 44.5cm) for the backing
- 1 rectangle 4″ × 13″ (10.2 × 33cm) for the hanging sleeve
- 4 rectangles 2″ × 15½″ (5.1 × 39.4cm) for the assembly
- 4 squares 4″ × 4″ (10.2 × 10.2cm) for the assembly

Shape-Flex

- 4 squares 9″ × 9″ (22.9 × 22.9cm)

Batting

- 1 square 17½″ × 17½″ (44.5 × 44.5cm)

Hanky

- Cut into 4 squares (right)

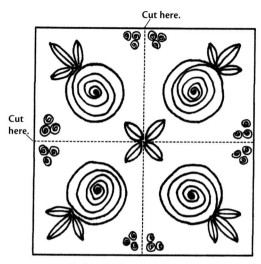

Hanky with design on all 4 corners

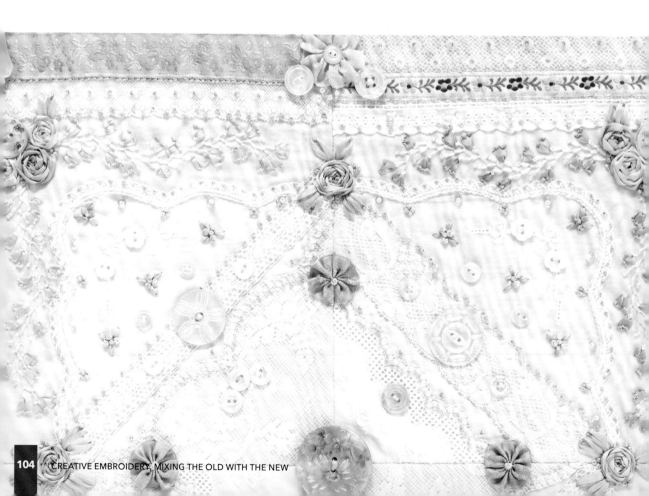

BLOCK COLLAGE

1. Fuse the interfacing to the wrong side of each fabric square 9″ × 9″ (22.9 × 22.9cm).

2. Follow the diagrams for each block, cutting the laces and ribbons to fit the square unless a specific measurement is given. Make 2 of each design.

- Place a hanky piece in the inner right corner.

- Place Lace A or G flush with the corner of the hanky and block.

- Place Lace B or H flush with the edges of Lace A or G.

- Place a 6½″ (16.5cm) length of Lace C or I ½″ (1.2cm) from the top edge.

- Cut a 6½″ (16.5cm) length of Lace D or J. Place Lace D 2″ (5.1cm) or Lace J 2½″ (6.4cm) from the top edge.

- Place a 6½″ (16.5cm) length of Ribbon M or O slightly over the 2 lace pieces.

- Place a 9″ (22.9cm) length of Lace E or L ½″ (1.2cm) from the left edge.

- Cut a 9″ (22.9cm) length of Lace F or K. Place Lace F 2½″ (6.4cm) or Lace K 2¾″ (7cm) from the left edge.

- Place a 9″ (22.9cm) length of ribbon N or P slightly over the 2 lace pieces.

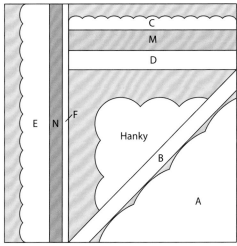

Block 1

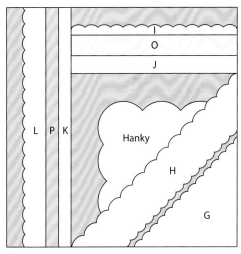

Block 2

3. Hand stitch the edges of the hankies, laces, and ribbons in place.

4. Arrange and sew the 4 blocks together in the order that they are shown, using a ¼″ (6mm) seam allowance.

Block assembly

EMBROIDERY AND EMBELLISHMENTS

Refer to the Visual Guide (page 6) for the page numbers of the embroidery stitches. See Materials for trim identification and abbreviations.

1. Draw or use the vine and rose pattern (right) as a guide. Work the stitches in the order listed below, using the suggested threads and embellishments. Stitch buttons in place with floss or perle cotton.

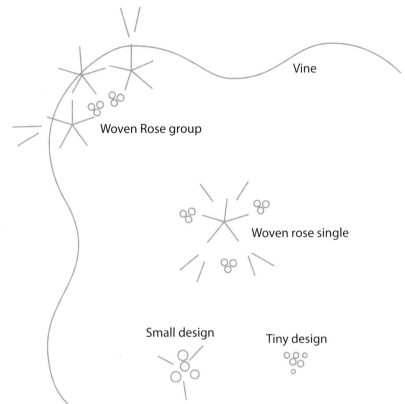

Vine

Woven Rose group

Woven rose single

Small design

Tiny design

- Vine: feather stitch, **SF**; 3 ribbon stitches with 4mm **SER** on tip, skip 1 tip, repeat; French knot stitch with **SF** at each tip

- Woven rose group and single: perle cotton and 7mm **SER**; lazy daisy stitch with 4mm **SER**; French knots with 2mm **SER**

- Small design: French knot stitch with 4mm **SER** and **SF**, straight stitch with 4mm **SER**

- Tiny design: French knot stitch with 2mm **SER** and **SF**

- Hanky: French knot stitch, **SF**; stem stitch, **SF**; stacked bead stitch, 6° and 11° **SB**; stacked bead stitch, novelty sequin and 15° **SB**; buttons

- C, D, E, F, I, J, K, L, lace edge suggestions: chain stitch, straight stitch; French knot stitch, **SF**; stacked bead stitch, novelty sequin and 15° **SB**; stacked bead stitch, 6° and 11° **SB**; buttons

- A and G lace edges: blanket stitch, **SF**; French knot stitch, **SF**; stacked bead stitch, novelty sequin and 15° **SB**; buttons

- B and H lace edges: straight stitch, French knot stitch **SF**; buttons

2. Make 4 rosettes (page 54) from ⅝" (1.6cm) rayon hem tape and ⅜" (1cm) satin ribbon. Hand stitch in place. Stitch a button or French knot stitch with 4mm SER in the center.

3. Stitch remaining buttons in place.

FINISHING

Hanging Sleeve

1. Fold and press the hanging sleeve rectangle in half lengthwise. Unfold and press under ¼" (6mm) on the short ends; machine stitch along the folds. Refold the piece.

2. Center and pin in place with the raw edges 2" (5.1cm) below the top edge of the backing and the folded edge extending up and beyond the backing.

3. Machine stitch the raw edges of the sleeve to the backing using a ¼" (6mm) seam.

4. Fold the sleeve down, enclosing the seam, and press flat. Hand stitch in place.

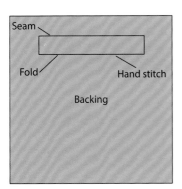

Hanging sleeve

Soft-Edge Assembly

1. Sandwich the batting in between the embroidered base and the backing.

2. Fold and press each fabric square 4" × 4" (10.2 × 10.2cm) into a triangle.

3. Fold and press under ⅜" (1cm) on one long edge of each rectangle 2" × 15½" (5.1 × 39.4cm); machine stitch along the folds.

4. Pin the raw edges of each triangle to the corners on the right side of the base.

5. With right sides together, pin the raw edges of the rectangles even with the edges of the base, leaving a 1" (2.5cm) space at each corner.

6. Machine stitch around the perimeter using a ⅜" (1cm) seam allowance. Trim the excess at the corners.

7. Turn the triangles to the backing, gently poking out the corners.

8. Press, pin, and hand stitch the finished edges of the rectangles to the backing.

9. Press, pin, and hand stitch the diagonal edge of the triangles to the backing.

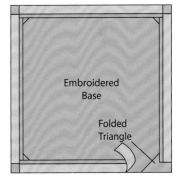

Pin the triangles and rectangles.

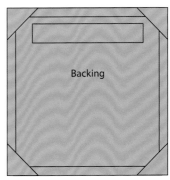

Hand stitch the rectangles and triangles in place.

Ribbons and Trims Squared

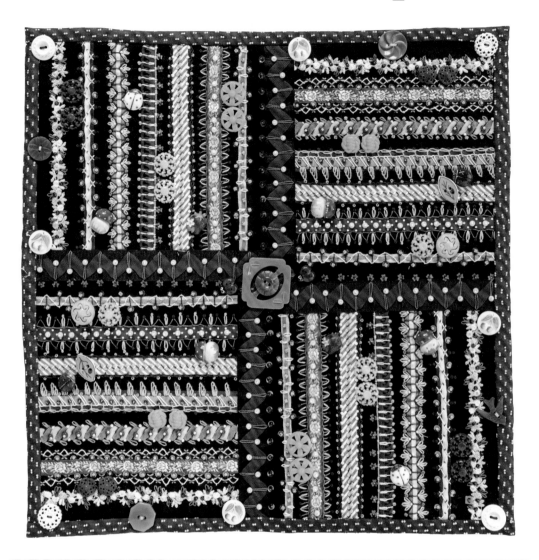

Size: 15″ × 15″ (38.1 × 38.1cm)

This project starts with 4 sections of a solid color fabric, each layered with a combination of ribbons and trims. The embroidery is worked in perle cotton, cotton floss, beads, and sequins, then embellished with a buckle and buttons.

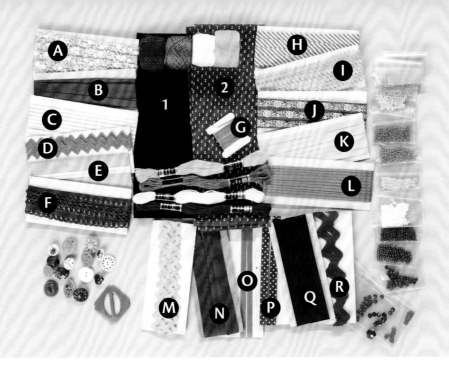

Materials

Fabric 1: ¾ yard (68.6cm) for the blocks and backing

Fabric 2: ¼ yard (22.9cm) for finishing

Perle cotton (PC) #8: 4 colors, 1 spool or skein each

Cotton floss (CF): 4 colors, 1 skein each

Ribbons and trims

A. Rococo trim: 1 yard (1m)

B. ⅜″ (1cm) satin ribbon: ½ yard (45.7cm)

C. ¼″ (6mm) ombré ribbon: ½ yard (45.7cm)

D. ⅜″ (1cm) rickrack: 1 yard (1m)

E. ⅛″ (3mm) satin ribbon: ½ yard (45.7cm)

F. ½″ (1.2cm) loop trim: ½ yard (45.7cm)

G. Knotting or rayon cord: ½ yard (45.7cm)

H. ½″ (1.2cm) bias binding: 1 yard (1m)

I. ¼″ (6mm) rickrack: 1 yard (1m)

J. ⅜″ (1cm) jacquard ribbon: 1 yard (1m)

K. ¼″ (6mm) satin ribbon: 1 yard (1m)

L. ⅛″ (3mm) satin ribbon: 2 yards (1.9m)

M. ⅜″ (1cm) rickrack: ½ yard (45.7cm)

N. ⅝″ (1.6cm) rayon hem tape: ½ yard (45.7cm)

O. ¼″ (6mm) satin ribbon: ½ yard (45.7cm)

P. ⅜″ (1cm) grosgrain ribbon: ½ yard (45.7cm)

Q. 1″ (2.5cm) grosgrain ribbon: 1 yard (1m)

R. ¾″ (1.9cm) rickrack: 1 yard (1m)

Buttons: 51 variety of sizes and styles

Seed beads (SB): small amounts

Size 6°: 2 colors

Size 8°: 1 color

Size 10°: 1 color vintage

Size 11°: 3 colors

Size 15°: 3 colors, 1 vintage

Sequins: 3 colors, 1 novelty in small amounts

Option: A similar size seed bead can be substituted for the vintage beads, and a standard sequin can be substituted for the novelty sequin.

Buckle 1½″ (3.8cm)

Pellon SF 101 Shape-Flex Interfacing: ½ yard (45.7cm)

Muslin: ½ yard (45.7cm)

Batting: ½ yard (45.7cm)

Sewing thread

Beading thread

Fabric glue stick

Cutting

Fabric 1

- 4 rectangles 8″ × 7″ (20.3 × 17.8cm) for the blocks
- 1 square 15″ × 15″ (38.1 × 38.1cm) for the backing

Fabric 2

- 1 rectangle 4″ × 13½″ (10.2 × 34.3cm) for the hanging sleeve
- 2 rectangles 3″ × 15″ (7.6 × 38.1cm) for the binding
- 2 rectangles 3″ × 17″ (7.6 × 43.2cm) for the binding

Shape-Flex

- 4 rectangles 8″ × 7″ (20.3 × 17.8cm)

1″ (2.5cm) grosgrain ribbon

- 4 lengths 8″ (20.3cm)

1″ (2.5cm) rickrack

- 4 lengths 8″ (20.3cm)

Muslin

- 1 square 15″ × 15″ (38.1 × 38.1cm)

Batting

- 1 square 15″ × 15″ (38.1 × 38.1cm)

BLOCK DESIGNS

1. Fuse the interfacing to the wrong side of each 8″ × 7″ (20.3 × 17.8cm) rectangle.

2. With a chalk pencil, mark 7 lines 1″ (2.5cm) apart across the 8″ (20.3cm) width of each block.

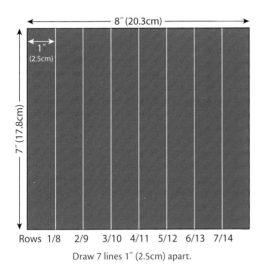

Rows 1/8 2/9 3/10 4/11 5/12 6/13 7/14

Draw 7 lines 1″ (2.5cm) apart.

3. Cut each trim 8″ (20.3cm) long, *unless otherwise noted*. Temporarily glue the trims in place.

4. Hand stitch the trims to the blocks following the block designs below. Make 2 of each block.

5. Trim off any excess ribbon or trim. Staystitch around the outer edges of the blocks.

Trim Placement and Embroidery Stitches

Refer to the Visual Guide (page 6) for the page numbers of the embroidery stitches. See materials for trim identification and abbreviations. Work the stitches in the order they are shown, using the suggested threads and embellishments.

BLOCK 1

- **Rows 1 and 8:** Trim A

  Embroidery: Lazy daisy stitch, **PC**; single bead stitch, 8° **SB**

- **Row 2:** Trims B and C

  Embroidery: Herringbone stitch, **PC**; straight and French knot stitches, **CF**; straight stitch, **CF**; stacked bead stitch, sequin and 11° **SB**

- **Row 3:** Trims D and E

  Embroidery: Fly stitch/long tail, **PC**; lazy daisy stitch, **CF**; French knot stitch, **PC**; single bead stitch, 15° **SB**

- **Row 4:** Trims F and G

  Stitches: Lazy daisy stitch/long arm, **PC**; couched stitch, **PC**; single bead stitch, 10° **SB**; stacked bead stitch, novelty sequin and 11° **SB**

- **Row 5:** Trims H and I

  Embroidery: Chain stitch double, **PC**; couched stitch, **CF**; French knot stitch, **CF**; single bead stitch, 11° **SB**

- **Row 6:** Trim J

  Embroidery: Blanket stitch, **PC**; fly stitch, **CF**; French knot stitch, **CF**; stacked bead stitch, 6° and 15° **SB**

- **Row 7:** Trims K and L knotted, see knotted ribbon (page 63)

  Embroidery: Lazy daisy stitch, **PC**; stacked bead stitch, sequin and 10° and 11° **SB**

BLOCK 2

- **Row 8:** See Row 1 (page 111).

- **Row 9:** Trim J

  Embroidery: Herringbone stitch **PC**; fly stitch, **PC**; straight stitch, **CF**; stacked bead stitch, sequin, and 11° **SB**

- **Row 10:** Trims D and M braided together, see detailed rickrack (page 63)

  Embroidery: Fly stitch offset, **PC**; lazy daisy stitch, **CF**; stacked bead stitch, 6° and 15° **SB**; stacked bead stitch, 10° and 15° **SB**

- **Row 11:** Trims N and O

  Embroidery: Blanket stitch, **PC**; blanket and chain stitches, **PC**; looped tendril stitch, **PC**; French knot stitch, **CF**; stacked bead stitch, 8° and 15° **SB**

- **Row 12:** Trims H and I

  Embroidery: Chain stitch spiny, **PC**; couched stitch, **CF**; single bead stitch, 11° **SB**

- **Row 13:** Trim P

  Embroidery: Blanket stitch closed, **PC**; lazy daisy with French knot stitch, **CF**; French knot stitch, **CF**; stacked bead stitch, 6° and 15° **SB**

- **Row 14:** Trims K and L couched using the couched stitch (page 74)

  Embroidery: Fly stitch, **PC**; straight stitch, **PC**; stacked bead stitch, sequin, 10°, and 11° **SB**

Base Assembly

1. Place the muslin square on top of the batting square.

2. Arrange and pin the blocks in place in the order that they are shown.

Note: *This will leave an open section in the center, which will be covered by ribbon.*

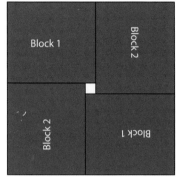

Arrange the blocks.

3. Hand stitch each piece of the 1″ (2.5cm) rickrack trim onto the 1″ (2.5cm) grosgrain ribbon pieces.

4. Pin a piece of ribbon over each vertical seam, then each horizontal seam, tucking under the raw edges at the center under the vertical pieces.

5. Hand stitch in place.

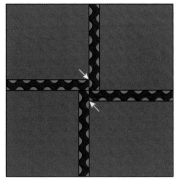

Hand stitch ribbon pieces in place.

6. Staystitch around the outer edges of the block.

7. Embroider: The rickrack with lazy daisy stitch, **PC**; stacked bead stitch, 6° and 15° **SB**; the ribbon edge with stacked bead stitch, novelty sequin, and 11° **SB**.

8. Stitch the buckle and buttons onto the blocks with **PC**.

FINISHING

Make and add a hanging sleeve (page 107) to the backing. To complete your artwork, stitch the remaining buttons along the edges once bound.

Bound Assembly

1. Sandwich the embroidered base and the backing with wrong sides together.

2. Fold and press the binding rectangles in half lengthwise.

3. Pin the shorter rectangles to the vertical edges of the base, right sides, and raw edges together.

4. Machine stitch using a ⅜″ (1cm) seam allowance.

5. Press the seam flat. Press and pin the folded edge to the backing. Hand stitch in place.

Bind the vertical edges.

6. Follow Steps 3–4 using the longer rectangles on the horizontal edges of the base. Follow Step 5, pressing and tucking in the raw edges at the ends first.

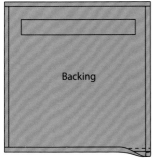

Bind the horizontal edges.

Signature Label

1. Cut 1 piece of light color fabric, backed with interfacing.

2. Cut the edges with pinking shears, or stitch lace, ribbon, or strips of fabric onto the raw edges.

3. Using a fabric marking pen, write the specifics of the artwork, including your name and those names and items that make this piece special.

4. Hand stitch this to the backing, with a tackstitch, running stitch, or embroidery stitch.

Two-Layer Quilting For projects that have a solid or pieced base, with batting added to the back, hand or machine stitch the base with perle cotton #12 or quilting thread.

STASH PROJECTS

The following pages are filled with ideas for you to use the precious treasures of this and that in your stash. There are *minimal instructions* so that your creative spirit can explore the possibilities. All the projects use a very small amount of fabric, in most cases less than a yard. The amounts for the additional materials will vary.

See Sewing Basics (page 141), Attaching Ribbon, Lace, and Trims to Fabric (page 52), Glossary of Hand-Sewn Stitches (page 52), Embroidery and Embellishment Stitches (page 70), and Embroidery Sketchbook (page 90).

Stash Idea Inspiration

A fast2fuse base covered with fabric, ribbon, and other trims can be embellished with gathered ephemera. See Heart Ornament or Pin (page 117).

A vintage wooden embroidery hoop becomes a frame for a precious scrap of lace, vintage mother-of-pearl buttons, and orphaned cufflinks. See Hoop Frame (page 136).

Love to Sew pin, 4½″ × 3¾″ (11.4 × 9.5cm)

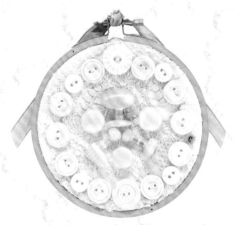

Auntie B's Finest, 4½″ × 4½″ (11.4 × 11.4cm)

A scrap of dyed silk fabric, a piece of crochet lace, and small appliqués, buttons, and beads become a gift for a friend. See Scrap Pins (page 133).

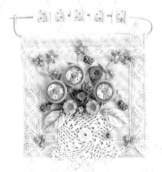

Aunt Murt's Garden, 4½″ × 5″ (11.4 × 12.7cm)

Table Runner

Featuring vintage feed sack and cotton fabrics, trims, and buttons

Collect from Stash

Muslin fabric: 1 yard (1m) for the base

Fabric: 1 yard (1m) for backing and binding

Batting: 1 yard (1m)

Feed sack fabric or other cotton prints:
Scraps to total ½ yard (45.7cm)

Rickrack: 8 yards (7.4m) total in a variety of widths

Ribbon: 1 yard (1m) lengths or more in a variety of widths

Embroidery threads: Perle cotton, cotton floss in a variety of colors

Embellishments: Buttons, sequins, charms, beads

Sewing thread

Beading thread

Cutting

See Base Center Piecing Chart (page 116) for additional sizes of muslin and fabric pieces.

Muslin

- 1 rectangle 6″ × 34½″ (15.2 × 87.6cm) for the base center
- 2 rectangles 2⅜″ × 34½″ (6 × 87.6cm) for the base borders

Fabric

- 1 rectangle 9¾″ × 34½″ (24.8 × 87.6cm) for the backing
- 2 rectangles 3″ × 34½″ (7.6 × 87.6cm) for the binding
- 2 rectangles 3″ × 11¾″ (7.6 × 29.8cm) for the binding

Muslin and fabric

- Cut the pieces following the center piecing chart.

Batting

- 1 rectangle 9¾″ × 34½″ (24.8 × 87.6cm)

BASE CENTER PIECING CHART			
Row (from top to bottom)	Muslin or print	Inches	Centimeters
Row 1	Muslin	6" × 2⅜"	15.2 × 6cm
Row 2	Print	6" × 3"	15.2 × 7.6cm
Row 3	Muslin	6" × 2"	15.2 × 5.1cm
Row 4	Print	6" × 2¾"	15.2 × 7cm
Row 5	Muslin	6" × 1½"	15.2 × 3.8cm
Row 6	Print	6" × 2⅛"	15.2 × 5.4cm
Row 7	Muslin	6" × 2"	15.2 × 5.1cm
Row 8	Print	6" × 3¼"	15.2 × 8.3cm
Row 9	Muslin	6" × 2"	15.2 × 5.1cm
Row 10	Print	6" × 2¾"	15.2 × 7cm
Row 11	Muslin	6" × 1⅜"	15.2 × 3.5cm
Row 12	Print	6" × 2"	15.2 × 5.1cm
Row 13	Muslin	6" × 2"	15.2 × 5.1cm
Row 14	Print	6" × 3⅜"	15.2 × 8.6cm
Row 15	Muslin	6" × 1¾"	15.2 × 4.4cm
Row 16	Print	6" × 2¾"	15.2 × 7cm
Row 17	Muslin	6" × 1½"	15.2 × 3.8cm
Row 18	Print	6" × 2¾"	15.2 × 7cm
Row 19	Muslin	6" × 2¼"	15.2 × 5.7cm

SEWING

1. Machine stitch the fabric and muslin pieces onto the muslin base center using a ¼" (6mm) seam allowance, following the above chart.

2. Pin the pieced base center to the middle of the batting.

3. Pin and machine stitch the muslin base borders to the pieced base center and batting.

Option: *Machine quilt the pieced base.*

Embroidery and Embellishments

1. Hand stitch the rickrack in place with sewing thread.

2. Embroider the rickrack with perle cotton and floss, using a variety of stitches.

3. Stitch the rosettes (page 54) from ribbon. Stitch into groups onto the base.

4. Stitch buttons, beads, and charms in place using a variety of stitches.

Detail of embroidery on rickrack trims

FINISHING

Follow the directions for Bound Assembly (page 113).

Heart Ornament or Pin

Featuring fabric,
vintage buttons, and lace

Size: 4½″ × 3¾″ (11.4 × 9.5cm)

Collect from Stash

Fabric

Pellon 911FF Fusible
Featherweight Interfacing

fast2fuse Double-sided
Heavyweight Fusible

Sewing thread

Felt

Buttons

Lace

Perle cotton

Tacky glue

For ornament: ⅜″
(1cm) satin ribbon

For pin: 2″ (5.1cm) pinback

Cutting

**Fabric (first backed with
interfacing)**

- 1 from Heart Ornament or Pin
  Pattern 1 (page 119)

fast2fuse

- 1 from Heart Ornament or Pin
  Pattern 2 (page 119)

Felt

- 1 from Heart Ornament or Pin
  Pattern 2 (page 119)

Lace and Pearl Pin

SEWING

1. Center the fast2fuse on the wrong side of the fabric; turn over and press the fabric to the fast2fuse.

2. Working from the back, clip the bottom tip and the top dip of the fabric close to the fast2fuse.

3. Thread a small sharps needle with sewing thread; knot the thread.

4. Fold over 1 edge at the bottom tip and tackstitch to the fast2fuse. Gather stitch along the fabric up to the top clip, ending with the needle on the right side of the fabric.

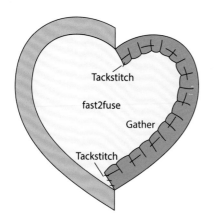

5. Gently pull the thread to gather the fabric around the edge of the fast2fuse. Tackstitch the raw edge of the fabric to the fast2fuse.

6. Repeat Steps 4 and 5 for the remaining edge.

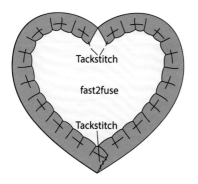

EMBROIDERY AND EMBELLISHMENTS

1. Pin and hand stitch a piece of lace, ribbon, or other trim onto the right side of the base, folding the raw edges to the wrong side.

2. Stitch buttons in place with perle cotton, using a variety of stitches.

3. Embroider the blanket stitch or blanket stitch up and down around the outer edge of the heart.

Option: *Work the French knot stitch off the tips of the blanket stitch.*

Finishing

1. Ornament: Cut 1 length of ribbon 4" (10.2cm). Fold the ribbon in half and stitch the raw edges to the fast2fuse.

Pin: Stitch the pinback to the felt piece.

2. Place a line of tacky glue around the outer edge of the felt piece. Press this to the back of the base.

Note: *Any size heart shape can be used. Just cut the fabric at least ¾" (1.9cm) larger than the fast2fuse base.*

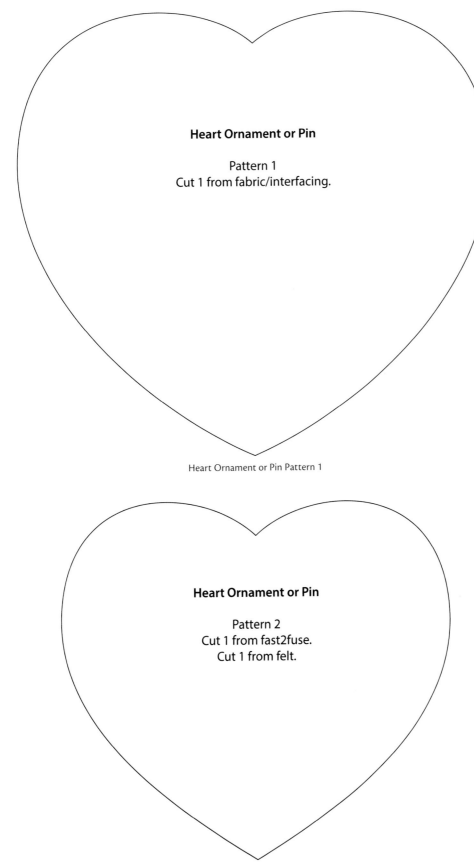

Heart Ornament or Pin

Pattern 1
Cut 1 from fabric/interfacing.

Heart Ornament or Pin Pattern 1

Heart Ornament or Pin

Pattern 2
Cut 1 from fast2fuse.
Cut 1 from felt.

Heart Ornament or Pin Pattern 2

HEART ORNAMENT OR PIN

Buckle Bookmarks

A   B

Featuring vintage fabrics, buttons, and buckles

Size: A. 2½″ × 8½″ (6.4 × 21.6cm)

B. 2½″ × 8¾″ (6.4 × 22.2cm)

Collect from Stash

Pellon 809 Décor-Bond Stabilizer

A piece of fabric or small scraps

Sewing thread

Embroidery threads: Perle cotton or cotton floss

Embellishments: Buckle, buttons

Lace or other trim

GENERAL DIRECTIONS

1. Cut 1 piece of Décor-Bond the width of the opening of the buckle and double the desired length of the bookmark.

2. Fabric options:

A. Cut a strip of fabric 1″ (2.5cm) wider and longer than the stabilizer. Hand stitch a piece of lace down the center.

B. Crazy-piece fabrics directly onto the stabilizer, ½″ (1.2cm) beyond all edges.

3. Embroider, using a variety of stitches. Stitch the buttons with perle cotton.

4. Press the raw edges of the fabric to the wrong side of the stabilizer, vertical then horizontal.

5. Machine or hand stitch around the folded edges.

6. Thread the base through the buckle and fold it in half, matching the bottom edges.

7. Hand stitch the folded edges together beginning and ending at the edge of the buckle.

Note: *Substitute a piece of ribbon for the fabric. In Step 1, cut the Décor Bond ⅛″ (3mm) narrower than the ribbon. Follow Steps 3, 4 (horizontal ribbon edge), 6, and 7.*

Tea Cozy

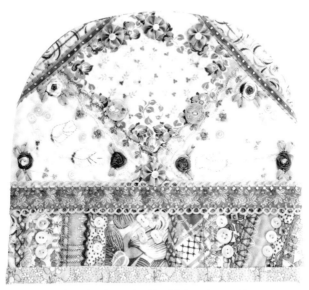

Front, featuring vintage hankies, fabrics, trims, and buttons

Back. Piece the front and back the same, or in a different pattern.

Size: 11″ × 9¼″ (27.9 × 23.5cm)

Collect from Stash

Hankies: 1 patterned, 3 embroidered

Muslin: ⅜ yard (34.3cm) for base

Fabric: ⅜ yard (34.3cm) for lining and binding

Fabric: Scraps totaling ¼ yard (22.9cm)

¾" (1.9cm) jacquard ribbon: 1 yard (1m)

½" (1.2cm) loop braid: 2 yards (1.9m)

⅜" (1cm) satin ribbon: 1 yard (1m)

⅛" (3mm) satin ribbon: 1½ yard (1.4m)

⅜" (1cm) grosgrain ribbon: 1 yard (1m)

Embroidery threads: Silk embroidery ribbon, perle cotton, cotton floss

Embellishments: Buttons, rosettes

Sewing thread

Cutting

Muslin

- 2 pieces using the Tea Cozy Pattern (page 124) for the front and back base
- 2 rectangles 3" × 12" (7.6 × 30.5cm) for the borders

Fabric

- 2 from Tea Cozy Pattern (page 124) for the lining
- 1 rectangle 3" × 22½" (7.6 × 57.2cm) for the binding

Note: *Cut the remaining pieces of fabric as you assemble the base and borders.*

Hanky

- Cut each hanky into 4 sections. See suggestions at right:

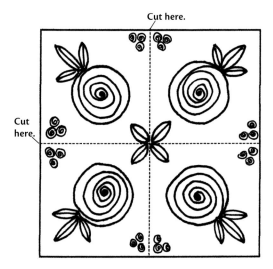

Cut a hanky that has an embroidered pattern on 1 or all 4 corners into 4 sections.

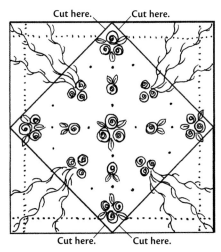

For a hanky that has an allover pattern, cut off each corner, leaving a square in the middle that can also be used in a collaged base.

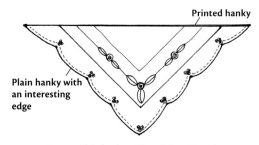

Layer a plain hanky with an interesting edge under a printed hanky edge.

SEWING

1. Strip- or crazy-piece the 2 muslin border pieces with the scrap fabrics.

2. Pin and machine stitch the border pieces on top of the lower edges of the front and back muslin base pieces. Cut off any excess fabric.

3. Collage piece the hankies above the borders, covering the rest of the muslin. Fill in any open areas with fabric scraps, layering any raw edge under a finished hanky edge, or cover with ⅜″ (1cm) satin ribbon.

4. Pin and hand stitch the hankies and fabric to the base pieces.

5. Stitch the loop braid and jacquard ribbons over the raw edges between the border and front and back pieces.

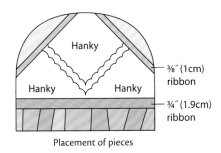

Placement of pieces

EMBROIDERY AND EMBELLISHMENTS

1. Pin and hand stitch the ⅛″ (3mm) satin ribbon to embellish.

2. Embroider the hankies, ribbons, and border section, using a variety of stitches.

3. Make rosettes (page 54) from the grosgrain ribbon. Stitch in place.

4. Stitch buttons in place with perle cotton.

Assembly

1. Pin and machine stitch the 2 embroidered base pieces together, using a ¼″ (6mm) seam allowance leaving the bottom edge open.

2. Open the embroidered base and press the edges.

3. Repeat Step 1 for the 2 lining pieces.

4. Insert the lining inside the embroidered base, wrong sides together.

5. Press the binding rectangle in half lengthwise.

6. Pin the raw edges of the binding and the base together, leaving ⅜″ (1cm) loose at the beginning and end.

7. Machine stitch with a ⅜″ (1cm) seam allowance.

8. Hand stitch the raw ends of the binding together; stitch the remaining section in place.

9. Press the folded edge over the seam allowance and to the lining. Hand stitch the folded edge to the lining.

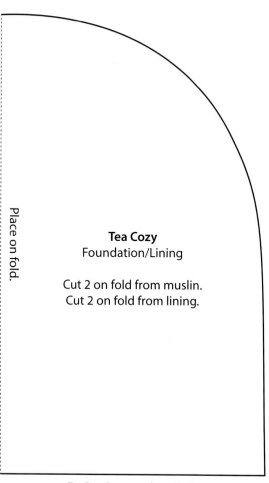

Place on fold.

Tea Cozy
Foundation/Lining

Cut 2 on fold from muslin.
Cut 2 on fold from lining.

Tea Cozy Pattern; enlarge 200%.

Doily Bunting

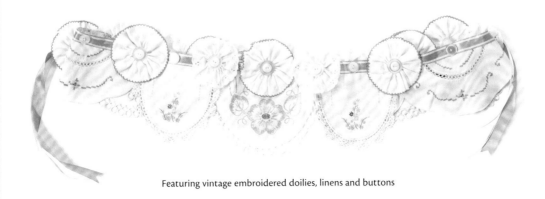

Featuring vintage embroidered doilies, linens and buttons

Size: 9″ × 120″ (22.9cm × 3.05m)

Collect from Stash

Doilies, small linens: 6 pieces in a variety of sizes; each cut in half

⅞″ (2.2cm) satin ribbon: 120″ (3.05m)

¼″ (6mm) satin ribbon: 2 lengths 120″ (3.05m) each

1½″ (3.8cm) cotton lace: 2 yards (1.9m)

2″ (5.1cm) cotton lace: 3½ yards (3.3m)

Embellishments: Buttons in a variety of sizes

Fabric glue stick

Perle cotton

Sewing thread

Detail of center section

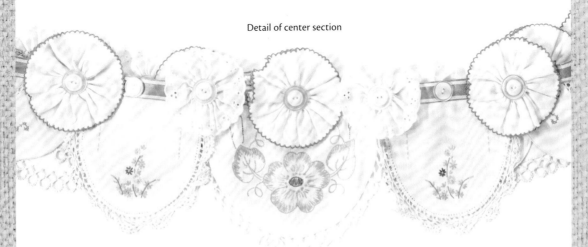

GENERAL DIRECTIONS

1. With the wider ribbon face down on a cutting mat, mark the center. Select a doily half for the center and 5 halves for each side.

2. Use a fabric glue stick to attach the doily right side down in the center of the wider ribbon, with the raw edge ⅛" (3mm) from the top selvage edge of the ribbon.

3. Layer and glue the next doily right side down slightly over the edge of the previous doily. Repeat for each doily, leaving a tail of ribbon on either end.

4. With the wider ribbon facing up, machine stitch a length of the narrower ribbon along the lower selvage edge of the wider ribbon, up to the edges of the doilies at the ends. Repeat this step for the upper selvage edge of the wider ribbon and the remaining length of the narrower ribbon.

5. Make rosettes (page 54) from the cotton laces. Stitch to the base of ribbons and doilies.

6. Stitch the buttons in place with perle cotton.

Did You Know?

Doilies

The term doily has been credited to a sixteenth-century London draper (cloth merchant) by the name of Doiley (or Doyley). Originally the term was used as an adjective that referred to a fancy napkin, and eventually as an ornamental covering for various surfaces.

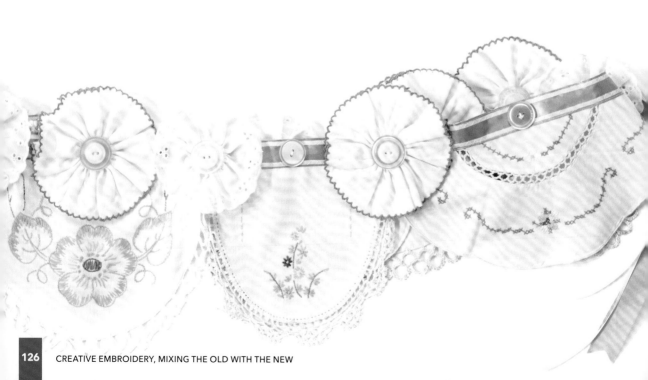

Hanky Bag

Featuring vintage hankies

Size: 3½″ × 3½″ (8.9 × 8.9cm)

Collect from Stash

Handkerchiefs: 2

⅜″ (1cm) satin ribbon: 2 yards (1.9m)

Sewing thread

DIRECTIONS

1. Place 2 hankies wrong sides together; pin the edges together.

2. Measuring from the center of each edge, draw the casing lines ½″ (1.2cm) apart. Machine stitch on the lines.

Insert ribbon.

Insert ribbon.

3. Cut 2 pieces of ribbon 1 yard (1m) each. Insert one piece into two adjacent sides of the casing. Repeat for the other piece of ribbon.

4. Pull the ribbon to gather the sections and to create the bag.

Framed Lace Collar

Featuring vintage lace collar, lace, glass and crochet buttons, and beads

Size: 13¾″ × 13¾″ (34.9 × 34.9cm)

Collect from Stash

Fabric A: ½ yard (45.7cm) solid fabric

Fabric B: ⅜ yard (34.3cm) printed fabric

Muslin: ½ yard (45.7cm)

Pellon SF 101 Shape-Flex Interfacing: ½ yard (45.7cm)

Batting: ½ yard (45.7cm)

Sewing thread

9″ (22.9cm) lace collar: 1

⅝″ (1.6cm) lace: 2 yards (1.9m)

⅜″ (1cm) satin ribbons: 2 yards (1.9m) each of 2 colors

Perle cotton

Silk embroidery ribbon: 4mm and 7mm

Embellishments: Buttons, flower shape beads, and 10mm beads

Beading thread

Cutting

Fabric A

- 1 square 9¾" × 9¾" (24.8 × 24.8cm) for the center
- 1 square 14¼" × 14¼" (36.2 × 36.2cm) for the backing
- 1 rectangle 4" × 11" (10.2 × 27.9cm) for the hanging sleeve

Fabric B

- 2 rectangles 2¼" × 9¾" (5.7 × 24.8cm) for the side borders
- 2 rectangles 2¾" × 14¼" (7 × 36.2cm) for the top and bottom borders
- 4 squares 4" × 4" (10.2 × 10.2cm) for the assembly
- 4 rectangles 2" × 11½" (5.1 × 29.2cm) for the assembly

Muslin

- 1 square 14¼" × 14¼" (36.2 × 36.2cm) for the base

Shape-Flex

- 1 square 14¼" × 14¼" (36.2 × 36.2cm) for the center

Batting

- 1 square 14¼" × 14¼" (36.2 × 36.2cm)

Satin ribbon

- 4 lengths from each color 14¼" (36.2cm)

Lace

- 4 lengths 14¼" (36.2cm)

SEWING

1. Fuse the interfacing to the muslin square.

2. Center the fabric square 10¼" × 10¼" (26 × 26cm) onto the muslin, right side up. Staystitch around the perimeter.

3. Pin and machine stitch border rectangles 2¾" × 10¼" (7 × 26cm) to the sides of the center. Press.

4. Pin and machine stitch border rectangles 2¾" × 14¼" (7 × 36.2cm) to the top and bottom of the center. Press.

5. Stitch 2 satin ribbons, 1 of each color, onto each side border, ½" (1.2cm) apart. Repeat for the top and bottom borders.

6. Center the lace over the inner edges of the ribbons on the side borders; hand stitch in place. Repeat with the lace on the top and bottom borders.

7. Hand stitch the collar onto the center.

Embroidery and Embellishments

1. Embroider the flowers and leaves with silk embroidery ribbon, French knot and straight stitches with perle cotton.

2. Embroider French knot stitches around the edges of the collar with perle cotton.

3. Stitch buttons in place with perle cotton.

4. Stitch beads in place.

Finishing

Follow the directions for the Hanging Sleeve (page 107) and the Soft-Edge Assembly (page 107).

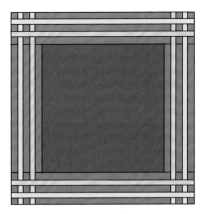

Lace Collage Brooch or Needle Keep

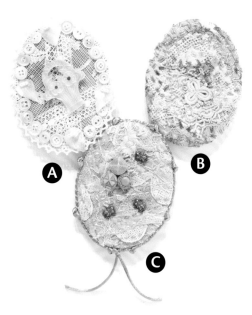

Featuring vintage lace, buttons, charms, and jewelry pin

Size: 2½″ × 3¼″ (6.4 × 8.3cm)

Collect from Stash

Fabric

Pellon 911FF Fusible Featherweight Interfacing

Scraps of lace

Sewing thread

fast2fuse Double-sided Heavyweight Fusible

Fabric glue stick

Batting

Felt

Tacky glue

Perle cotton

Sewing thread

Beading thread

Embellishment options: Buttons, leaf and flower charms, size 11° seed beads, jewelry pin, large buttons, rayon cord

For brooch: 1½″ (3.8cm) pinback

Cutting

Fabric (first backed with interfacing)

- 1 from Pattern 1 (page 132)

fast2fuse

- 1 from Pattern 2 (page 132)

Batting

- 1 from Pattern 2 (page 132)

Felt

- 1 from Pattern 2 (page 132) for the brooch

Or

- 3 from Pattern 2 (page 132) for the needle keep

ASSEMBLY

1. Collage and layer the lace pieces onto the fabric base; hand stitch in place.

Note: *If you are using small scraps of lace, temporarily glue these in place first with a fabric glue stick.*

2. Trim ⅛″ (3mm) from the edges of the batting. Center and iron to the fast2fuse.

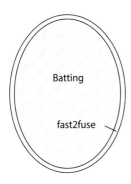

3. Thread a small sharps needle with sewing thread and knot the thread.

4. Stitch a basting stitch ¼″ (6mm) from the raw edge of the fabric.

5. Place the batting side of the fast2fuse on top of the interfaced side of the fabric.

6. Pull the thread to gather the stitches. Tackstitch; knot and cut the thread.

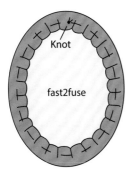

7. Press the front of the base. Press the fabric edges on the back.

Embroidery and Embellishments

A. Stitch a narrow lace around the outer edge. Stitch the buttons with perle cotton; stitch the charms with beads. Place a jewelry pin in the center.

B. Embroider the seed stitch and French knot stitches with perle cotton.

C. Embroider running and straight stitches with perle cotton. Stitch the buttons and charms with sewing thread. Couch a rayon cord around the outer edge with perle cotton.

FINISHING

1. Place a line of tacky glue around the outer edge of a piece of felt. Press onto the back of the fabric.

2. Brooch: Stitch the pinback to the felt. **OR:** Needle Keep: Whipstitch 2 pieces of felt together. Tackstitch the top portion of the stitched edge to the glued piece of felt.

Lace Collage Brooch or Needle Keep

Pattern 1
Cut 1 from fabric/interfacing.

Pattern 1

**Lace Collage Brooch
or
Needle Keep**

Pattern 2
Cut 1 from fast2fuse.
Cut 1 from batting.
Cut 1 or 3 from felt.

Pattern 2

Scrap Pins

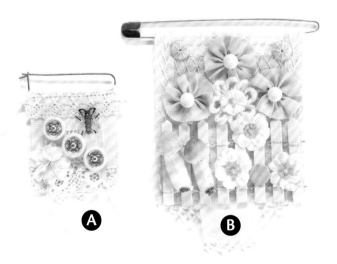

A

B

Collect from Stash

Pellon SF 101 Shape-Flex Interfacing

Scraps of fabric, laces, trims, ribbons

Embroidery threads: Perle cotton or cotton floss

Embellishments: Ephemera

Knitting or laundry pin

Sewing thread

Optional: Glue stick

Featuring vintage knitting or laundry pins, lace, trims, and embellishments

Size: A. 2½″ × 3″ (6.4 × 7.6cm) B. 5½″ × 6″ (14 × 15.2cm)

GENERAL DIRECTIONS

1. Measure the width of the pin. Determine the desired length, then add 1″ (2.5cm) to the top. Cut the interfacing this measurement. Place the fusible side up.

2. Collage and cover the interfacing base with bits of fabric, ribbon, lace, and trims. Fuse in place.

3. Press 1″ (2.5cm) to the wrong side to create the casing. Glue or hand stitch in place.

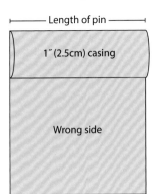

Length of pin

1″ (2.5cm) casing

Wrong side

4. Embroider and embellish as desired with perle cotton and floss.

5. Insert the pin into the casing.

Note: *You could substitute a wide length of ribbon for the interfacing. Follow from Step 2, temporarily gluing the pieces in place first with a glue stick.*

Button Garland

Collect from Stash

1″ (2.5cm) grosgrain ribbon: 2 pieces 92″ (2.37m) each

⅝″ (1.6cm) twill tape: 92″ (2.37m)

Buckles: 11 in a variety of sizes

Button: 11 shank buttons, 70 or more sew-through buttons

Perle cotton

Sewing thread

Optional: Seed beads and beading thread

GENERAL DIRECTIONS

1. Thread the twill tape through the buckles.

2. Pin the twill tape onto the grosgrain ribbon, spacing the buckles at even intervals, leaving an 8″ (20.3cm) tail at both ends.

3. Hand stitch the tape in place with sewing thread or perle cotton.

4. Hand stitch the buckles in place with perle cotton. Stitch a shank button in the center of each buckle.

5. Stitch 7 or more sew-through buttons between the buckles with perle cotton.

Option: *Stack a smaller button on top of a larger button. Stitch beads through the holes of the buttons and the open spaces between buttons.*

6. Use sewing thread or perle cotton to hand stitch the remaining ribbon onto the back of the base, from the first to the last buckle.

Featuring vintage buttons and buckles

Size: 1½″ × 92″ (3.8cm × 2.35m)

Treasure Keeper Pocket

Featuring vintage ribbons, lace, and buttons

Size: 3″ × 4¾″ (7.6 × 12.1cm)

Collect from Stash

3″ (7.6cm) grosgrain ribbon: 9½″ (24.1cm) for the base

Pellon SF101 Shape-Flex Interfacing: 2¾″ × 9½″ (7 × 24.1cm)

Fabric: 2¾″ × 9″ (7 × 22.9cm) for the lining

Buttons: A variety of sizes

Trims:

A. 1 piece ⅝″ (1.6cm) jacquard ribbon and 2 pieces ⅜″ (1cm) grosgrain ribbon: 9½″ (24.1cm) each

B. 2¼″ (5.7cm) lace and ⅜″ (1cm) grosgrain ribbon: 9½″ (24.1cm) each

Perle cotton

Sewing thread

GENERAL DIRECTIONS

1. Fuse the interfacing to the wrong side of the grosgrain ribbon base.

2. Decorate the surface:

A. Machine or hand stitch the jacquard and grosgrain ribbons in place.

B. Hand stitch the lace in place, then the grosgrain ribbon over the lace. Embroider with the blanket stitch.

3. Stitch buttons with perle cotton or sewing thread.

4. Pin the wrong side of the lining even with the raw edges of the ribbon base. Machine or hand stitch using a ¼″ (6mm) seam allowance.

5. Open, then press the seam towards the ribbon.

6. Fold the pocket in half; hand stitch the sides together.

Hoop Frame

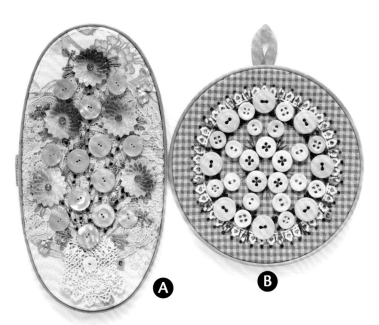

A

B

Featuring vintage embroidery hoop, fabric, lace, and buttons

Collect from Stash

Fabric

Pellon 911 Featherweight Interfacing

Note: *Use one piece of fabric or piece sections together, then fuse the interfacing to the wrong side.*

Embroidery hoop

    A. 9″ × 5″ (22.9 × 12.7cm)

    B. 6¼″ (15.9cm) in diameter

Pearl cotton

Sewing thread

Felt

Fray Check

Tacky glue

⅜″ (1cm) ribbon: 4″ (10.2cm)

Embellishment options:

    A. 5½″ (14cm) doily, 1½″ × 1½″ (3.8 × 3.8cm) section of lace for basket, buttons, and charms

    B. ⅜″ (3.8cm) lace, and buttons

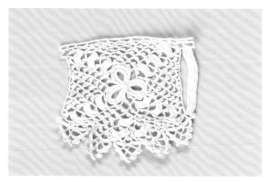

Use a section of lace for a basket, place a line of Fray Check across the raw edges.

GENERAL DIRECTIONS

1. Cut 1 circle of fabric 2" (5.1cm) larger than the outer edges of the embroidery hoop.

2. Cut the felt the same size as the inner section of the embroidery hoop.

3. Following Design A below or B right, hand stitch elements in place with sewing thread.

4. Machine staystitch ¼" (6mm) from the raw edges of the fabric.

5. Apply Fray Check to the raw edges.

6. Place the fabric in the embroidery hoop. Pull the fabric taut.

7. Follow Design A below or B right to embroider and embellish.

Design A

1. Stitch the doily in place, then the lace for the basket.

2. Draw the lines for the stems and leaves.

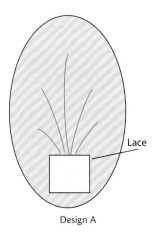

Design A

3. Embroider the feather stitch on the lines, stitch straight stitches for additional stalks, add French knot stitches, and lazy daisy stitches for details. Stitch the buttons and charms in place with perle cotton.

Design B

1. Draw a 4" (10.2cm) circle on the center of the fabric. Stitch the lace on the circle.

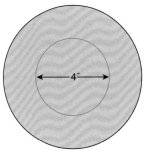

Design B

2. Stitch the buttons with perle cotton. Embroider straight stitches and French knot stitches around the buttons.

FINISHING

1. Thread a small sharps needle with sewing thread, doubled; knot the ends.

2. Fold under the raw edges of the fabric at the staystitch line. Gather stitch along the folded edges.

3. Gently pull the thread to gather the stitches. Tackstitch, knot and cut the thread.

4. Fold the ribbon in half. Stitch or glue the raw edges onto the fabric back.

5. Glue the felt to the fabric back.

Alternate Foundation Substitute a circle or oval cut from fast2fuse for the hoop. Cut a piece of batting ⅛" (3mm) smaller, the fabric backed with interfacing 2" (5.1cm) larger, and the felt the same size as the fast2fuse. Follow Steps 3–7 of Assembly (page 131) and Step 1 of Finishing (page 131) for the Lace Collage Brooch or Needle Keep.

UPcyCleD Jell-O Mold

Featuring vintage aluminium mold, fabric, and buttons

Size: 3½″ × 2¼″ (8.9 × 5.7cm)

Collect from Stash

Jell-O mold

Option: *A teacup or sugar bowl can replace the mold.*

Fabric backed with Pellon 911 Featherweight Interfacing

Lace

Sewing thread

Stuffing

Tacky glue

GENERAL DIRECTIONS

1. Measure the diameter of the opening of the mold. Cut 1 fabric circle (backed with interfacing) twice the measurement.

2. Glue lace around the inside edge of the mold.

Option: *Embellish the fabric with a doily or buttons.*

3. Stitch a running stitch around the raw edge of the fabric circle; gather slightly.

4. Fill with stuffing. Pull the stitches tightly. Tackstitch, knot and cut the thread.

5. Glue the gathered side of the stuffed fabric circle into the mold.

Two molds, 1 for the pincushion and 1 for a bowl, with a wooden spool pedestal, and a mat made from penny circles (page 68). Size: 3½″ in diameter × 4″ (8.9 × 10.2cm).

Vase of Flowers

Featuring vintage creamer, trims, buttons, and notions

Size: 5½″ × 6½″ (14 × 16.5cm)

Collect from Stash

Vase: China creamer, teacup, sugar bowl, or other container

Various widths of ribbon: Double-faced satin, grosgrain, velvet, satin print. See specific flower directions for lengths needed.

12″ (30.5cm) zipper: 1 flower color and 1 green

Sewing thread

Felt

Embellishments: Buttons, 1 for each flower

18-gauge florist wire: 1 package

Tacky glue

Styrofoam ball: Same diameter as the inside bottom of the container

Flower Suggestions

Stitch each of the following flowers. Sew a button into each.

1. Rosette (page 54)

2. Double rosette (page 56)

3. Fancy flowers, posy (page 54) using layered inner edge ribbon directions (page 53)

4. Loop leaf (page 60), 8RW

5. Zipper rose (page 59), 6″ (15.2cm)

   Not Shown: Zipper leaf (page 60), 4″ (10.2cm)

GENERAL DIRECTIONS

1. Cut a 1" (2.5cm) circle of felt for each flower.

2. With wire cutters, cut the florist wire into a variety of stem lengths, longer than the height of the container.

3. With pliers, fold 1 end of the wire stem into a spiral; bend the spiral 90° to the stem. Glue the spiral to the wrong side of the flower.

4. Cut a small slit in each felt circle; insert the stem into the slit and bring it to the wrong side of the flower. Glue in place.

5. Glue the leaves to the wrong side of the flower.

6. Cut the Styrofoam ball in half. Glue the flat side into the center of the container.

7. Arrange and place the flower stems into the Styrofoam.

Wire guide

Wooden Spool Vase

Featuring vintage wooden spool, ribbon, zipper, and buttons

Size: 1½" × 5½" (3.8 × 14cm)

1. Follow the directions for the rosette (page 54), or any other flower.

2. Follow Steps 1–4 of General Directions for Vase of Flowers (page 139) to attach the stems.

3. Glue a zipper to the base of the wooden spool and decorate with a button.

4. Arrange the flower stems into the opening of the spool.

Option: *Add vintage beaded or paper floral leaves.*

Sewing Basics

SEWING TOOLS

You should have a sewing machine, iron, ironing board, and a pressing mat all in good working condition in addition to the following items.

1. E6000 Adhesive, to attach metal or glass items

2. 6″ clear ruler with ⅛″ and ¼″ markings

3. 18″ quilter's ruler

4. Chalk pencil

5. Fabric glue stick

6. Fray Check, used on fabric, lace, and ribbon to keep the edges from fraying

7. Nonstick pressing sheet

8. Rotary cutter

9. Rotary mat

10. Seam ripper

11. Sewing thread

12. Straight pins

13. Scissors, fabric, and craft

14. Tacky Glue, to attach small fiber items

15. Wooden stuffing tool

Sulky KK 2000 Temporary Spray Adhesive, to temporarily adhere fabrics together while piecing (not shown)

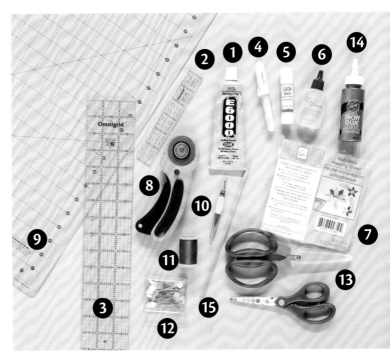

Stash Idea Inspiration

You will find a myriad of free projects on C&T Publishing's website, including this needle keep. Go to ctpub.com and click on the link Free Projects.

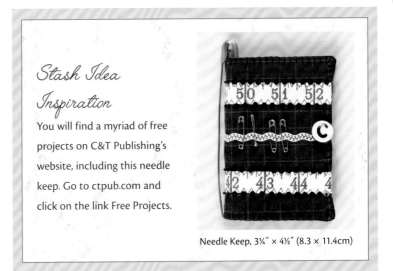

Needle Keep, 3¼″ × 4½″ (8.3 × 11.4cm)

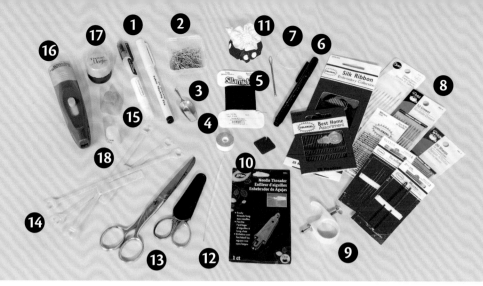

HAND-STITCHING TOOLS

These are the basic tools to keep on hand for hand stitching small items, embroidery, and embellishment.

1. Air-erasable or water-soluble pens

2. Appliqué pins, for trims or appliqués

3. Bead scoop for picking up loose beads

4. Beading thread: Nymo and Silamide

5. Bodkin, to thread ribbon through eyelet lace

6. Fabric marking pen, to mark or add your name to your project

7. Needle grabber, to pull the needle through layers of fabric

8. Needles: beading, chenille, cotton darner, crewel, embroidery, milliner, plastic large-eye needle, small sharps

9. Needle puller

10. Needle threaders

11. Pincushion

12. Porcupine quill or cocktail straw for use in silk ribbon embroidery

13. Scissors: embroidery, craft

14. Stitch Bow organizers, to keep floss from tangling

15. Synthetic beeswax, to condition beading thread

16. Thread Zapper, a battery-powered tool with a heated element to melt the edges of synthetic-fiber ribbon to prevent fraying

17. Thread Magic conditioner, to minimize knotting of embroidery and sewing threads

18. Thimble

Needle-nose pliers and wire cutters, to use on florist wire (not shown)

Which Needle?

- Beading: Use with beading threads.

- Chenille: Use for silk embroidery ribbon or a group of twisted threads.

- Cotton darner: Use for twisted threads.

- Crewel: Use for twisted threads.

- Embroidery: Use for stranded floss.

- Plastic large-eye: Use for weaving wide ribbons.

- Sharps: Use for hand sewing.

Note: *Special thanks to Colonial Needle company for providing the needles shown above and the perle cotton used throughout the samples.*

BASIC SEWING INSTRUCTIONS

See a Glossary of Hand-Sewn Stitches (page 52) for basic stitch terminology, and Attaching Ribbon, Lace, and Trims to Fabric (page 52) for basic hand-stitching directions.

- Prewash cotton fabrics to eliminate chemicals and to prevent shrinkage or bleeding.

- Draw around the outer edges of a pattern with an Air Erasable pen.

- Use Sulky KK 2000 Temporary Spray Adhesive to keep the fabric pieces in a collage base in place. For smaller pieces of ribbon, lace, or trims, use a fabric glue stick.

- For a project that has a pieced base, use a ¼" (6mm) seam allowance unless otherwise noted.

- When using a fusible stabilizer, follow the manufacturer's instructions.

- When machine stitching, do not backstitch at the beginning and end of a pieced seam, as this adds bulk to the sections that you will embroider.

- To prevent the finished fabric base from fraying, serge or zigzag around the edges. For ribbons, trims, and lace, apply a thin line of Fray Check on the raw edges.

EMBROIDERY AND EMBELLISHMENT BASICS

See Embroidery and Embellishment Stitches (page 70) for directions and refer to the Visual Guide (page 6) for the page numbers of the embroidery stitches.

- When working with a skein of floss, cut off the length of thread, then split the threads into the number that you want to work with. Separate each thread individually from the group; then reassemble these back together to eliminate tangling.

- When working with a skein of perle cotton, I suggest cutting through the knot and the entire skein to create separate lengths. Loop the threads over a ring and tie into a loose knot. Remove one length of thread and cut it in half so that you have a shorter length.

- When embroidering with silk embroidery ribbons, in most cases the ribbon should lie flat against the fabric. However, the ribbon can twist once it is pulled through the fabric. If the ribbon is concave, hold the ribbon next to the fabric then stitch. If the ribbon is convex, rub the ribbon until it is flat, or concave.

- Stitch buttons and found objects to the base of your project using sewing thread, floss, or perle cotton.

- Nymo and Silamide beading threads are used double, with a knot in the ends. Synthetic beeswax will hold the threads together.

- Do not stitch beads, buttons, or charms close to the raw edges; leave about ⅝" (1.6cm) allowance.

Important Note: *This author acknowledges that there may be some inexactness in the metric conversions. I recommend that you refer to online converters if more exact measurements are desired.*

Gallery and More Inspiration

Linen and Lace Wall Pocket

12" × 23½" (30.5 × 59.7cm)

The printed linen base is a backdrop for three pockets, each a compilation of table linens, layered doilies, appliqués, laces, and ribbon. Embellishments include ribbonwork flowers, buttons, charms, and celluloid pins. See Flowers and Leaves (page 54), and Custom Hanger (page 101) for ideas.

Buttons and Buckles Pin

3¾" × 5" (9.5 × 12.7cm)

The base of this pin is a fast2fuse shape covered with grosgrain ribbon. It is adorned with mother-of-pearl and celluloid buttons, buckles, zipper, and twill tape flowers. See Flowers and Leaves (page 54) for ideas.

Did You Know?

Design Secrets

There was extreme competition among lacemaking regions, each region keeping the techniques and designs a secret. Many lace-makers spent their entire lives making only one part of a lace pattern, such as a flower, and never saw the complete design.

Grandmother's Fans by Diane Herbort

27″ × 27″ (68.6 × 68.6cm)

The fans are cut from old dresser scarves, with a crazy pieced background made from genuine and reproduction 1930s fabrics. The embroidery is worked in both solid and hand-dyed perle cotton, with additional embroidery added to the fans. Embellishments include vintage lace and crochet pieces, plastic and mother-of-pearl buttons, and silver snaps.

Rustic Americana

13½″ × 10″ (34.3 × 25.4cm)

The flag design was stitched together with left-over fabrics both vintage and new, vintage seam binding, and a collection of vintage and new heart and star buttons. See Firm-Back Assembly (page 101) for base and finishing ideas.

Complementary Mystic

8½″ × 9½″ (21.6 × 24.1cm)

The base was created with batik fabric, vintage jacquard ribbons, and hand-dyed ribbons using Colorhue dyes, and embellished with bead embroidery, sequins, and buttons. See Dyeing to be Beautiful (page 49), and Custom Hanger (page 101) for ideas.

Ugly Bug Ball

7″ (17.8cm) in diameter

A piece of cotton twill fabric with a web design made from vintage embroidery ribbon and rickrack trims holds host to this collection of "ugly bugs" stitched mainly from old sewing notions. See Hoop Frame (page 136), and Steampunk Bugs (page 88) for ideas.

Sundries Sampler by Nancy Karst

8" × 5" (20.3 × 12.7cm)

These two sections are part of a booklet that was created with a salesman's samples of wool swatches purchased at an antique mall. The designs include vintage pieces of lace, trims, doilies, and yo-yos, and are embroidered and embellished with threads, beads, charms, and vintage buttons.

Scattered Splattered Tatters

13″ × 13″ (33 × 33cm)

Left-over pieces of muslin fabric were crazy-pieced together, then hand quilted with perle cotton #12. Crochet and mother-of-pearl buttons are nestled into the lengths of tatted and machine-made lace, scattered crochet, and tatted appliqués. The finished piece was hand-dyed using Colorhue dyes. See Rustic Aging (page 50) for ideas.

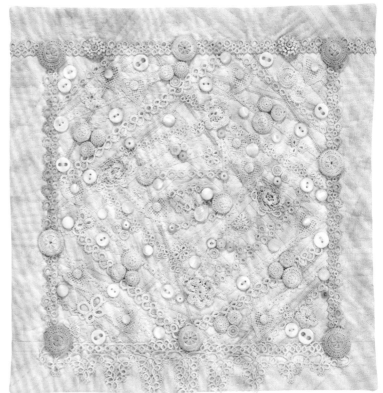

Scrapped Memories

2¼″ × 28½″ (5.7 × 72.4cm)

A wide length of ribbon was pieced with scrap bits of fabric, lace, and trims, and adorned with rosettes, yo-yos, embroidery, buttons, charms, and beads. See Flowers and Leaves (page 54) and Little Stitched Extras (page 65) for ideas.

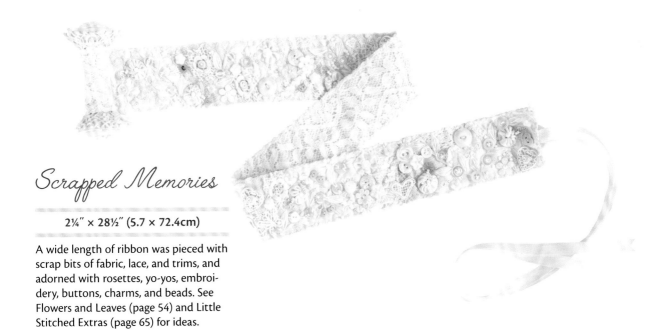

Sweet Dreams

24" × 20" (61 × 50.8cm)

The vintage embroidered piece, a gift from a friend, is framed with strip- and crazy-pieced borders of feed sack fabrics and cotton prints. Embellishments include rickrack trim, cotton hem tape, grosgrain ribbon, ribbonwork flowers, rickrack flowers, yo-yos, doilies, and vintage and new buttons. See Altering the Past (page 47) for ideas.

A Note from the Author

A key factor to any project, whether simple or complex, is the level of time and commitment that you can give yourself to complete it. Be mindful and give yourself room to learn and grow.

Butterfly Fields

23″ × 19″ (58.4 × 48.3cm)

An old Battenburg lace doily was cut into sections to form the three trees that are stitched to a batik background framed with a strip-pieced border. Embellishments include ribbonwork and lace flowers, beads, sequins, buttons, and charms. See Flowers and Leaves (page 54) for ideas.

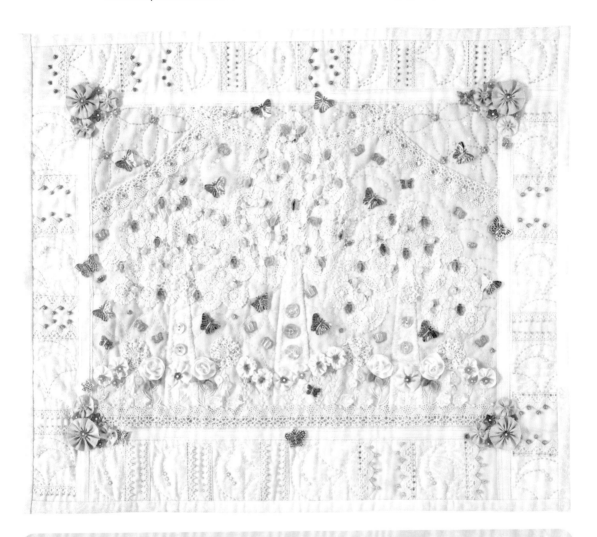

Did You Know?

Brides and Bridges

The little groups of threads connecting the main designs of lace (such as flowers or scrolls) are known as brides, bridges, bars, or legs.

Old School Family Guys

11¼″ × 14½″ (28.6 × 36.8cm)

This pieced log-cabin-style base began with an elongated center to highlight a silk ribbon that was found in one of my grandfather's drawers. I dedicated this to our families' guys: Thurston, William, Peter, George, Delbert, Richard, and my guy Kevin. Each with an initial charm surrounded by their hobbies, also included are a variety of buttons and vintage advertising pins. See Custom Hanger (page 101) for ideas.

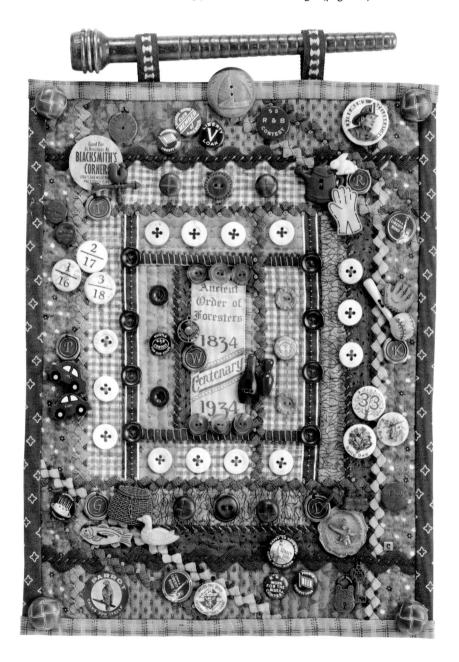

Vintage Sewing Collection

Sewing Kit, 3½″ × 5″ (8.9 × 12.7cm) and Needle Keep, 3¼″ × 4½″ (8.3 × 11.4cm).

This sewing kit and needle keep were stitched from a scrap of vintage flannel fabric. The embellishments include a vintage measuring tape, soutache trim, woven rickrack, buttons, sequins, beads, and sewing notions. Also shown are a collection of well-loved vintage sewing tools.

Measured Party Fowl

20½″ × 16½″ (52.1 × 41.9cm)

A machine quilted base of pieces of left-over fabrics and a gifted bag full of selvage edge strips becomes the background for a collection of whimsical friends. An old tape measure was used for the body of each bird, with fun googly eyes, rickrack legs, laundry pin wings, shoe beads, and hat buttons. Other embellishments are rickrack and ribbon-work flowers, vintage buttons, glass mushrooms, vintage tin pins, and metal charms. The birds were inspired by a Free Mug Rug Project, designed by Jenifer Dick, found on C&T's website.

Well Hello Dolly

17" × 22" (43.2 × 55.9cm)

Vintage jacquard ribbons from the 1940s frame the four hand-quilted, printed pattern pieces for the dolls, Alice and Jeannie. Embellishments include a leaf trim, ribbonwork flowers, celluloid flower pins, glass beads, and vintage hat buttons. See Flowers and Leaves (page 54) for ideas.

Did You Know?

Jacquard Ribbons

Jacquard ribbons are woven on special looms that use a series of punch cards to raise and lower warp threads. These designs create varied textures and intricate patterns on the surface while leaving long warp threads on the reverse side.

Jacquard Ribbon Projects

1. Treasure Keeper Pocket (page 135)
2. Buckle Bookmarks (page 120)

Pistachio Moss

19½″ × 21½″ (49.5 × 54.6cm)

The pieced background is worked around a center section of silk charmeuse and several pieces of vintage lace and appliqués that were dyed using Colorhue dyes. Ribbonwork flowers and leaves were made from Hannah silk bias ribbons, with additional ribbons and laces also dyed with the Colorhue dyes. See Dyeing to be Beautiful (page 49) for ideas.

Kimono Ties

15″ × 15″ (38.1 × 38.1cm)

The crazy-pieced and machine quilted base is comprised of silk fabrics, men's ties, and pieces of kimonos, haoris, and obis. The embellishments include vintage glass, celluloid, and inlaid buttons, fabric yo-yos, fabric circles, and embroidery. See Little Stitched Extras (page 65) for ideas.

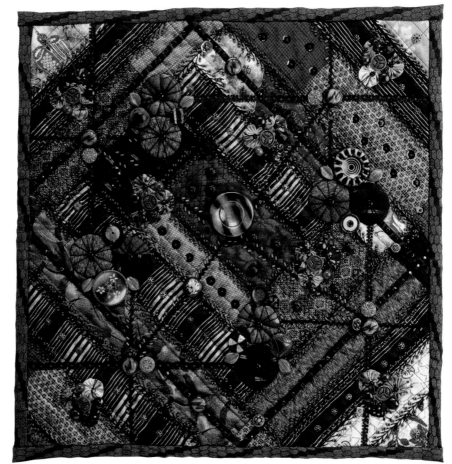

Mary Margaret's Pretty Purse

7½″ × 8½″ (19.1 × 21.6cm)

The pieced base of silk ties and a scrap of silk fabric features a small purse with steel cut beads and a metal frame. Embellishments include silk ribbon and ribbonwork embroidery, vintage gimp and rickrack trims, fabric, metal, crochet, and glass buttons, and glass beads. See Alternate Foundation (page 137) to create the base.

Bees Buzz on a Saturday Afternoon

26¾" × 22½" (67.9 × 57.2cm)

This patch- and strip-pieced grouping of cotton prints and vintage printed panels, with layered vintage rickrack trims, jacquard, and grosgrain ribbons, becomes the backdrop for a medley of vintage and new buttons, scatter pins, birds' nests, and ribbonwork flowers. See Altering the Past (page 47) for ideas.

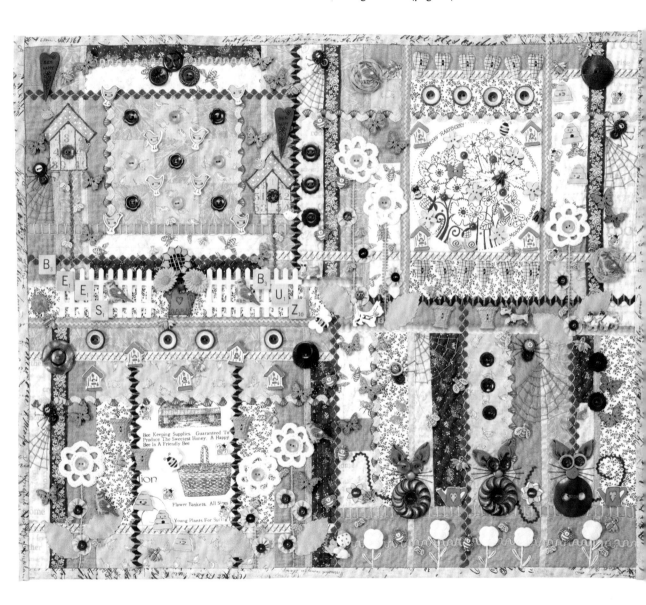

About the Author

Christen Brown first became interested in arts and crafts as a child and teenager, immersing herself in classes that explored creative endeavors including drawing, painting, ceramics, jewelry making, and sewing.

Christen's wearable art has been shown in galleries and fashion shows all over the world. She began teaching and presenting her work with the hopes to inspire and encourage future creative minds. She began writing articles for magazines in 2010, then moved to writing books in 2011.

Christen's titles for C&T Publishing include *Ribbonwork Gardens, Embroidered and Embellished, Ribbonwork Flowers, The Embroidery Book, Beaded Embroidery Stitching,* and *Hand Embroidery Dictionary.* Her other products include *Embroidery*

Stitching Handy Pocket Guide, Embroidery Stencils Essential Collection, Embroidery Stencils the Darling Motif Collection, Embellished Art Embroidery Project Planner, and *Embroidery Stencils Crazy Quilt Seam Design Collection.*

Christen continues to be interested in creating and experimenting, specifically concentrating on technique and design of embroidery, quilting, ribbonwork, mixed media, and beadwork. Her goal is to continually grow, be surprised, and be inspired, and create new and relevant pieces.

She works and teaches out of her home studio in Escondido, California.

Visit Christen online!

Website:
christenbrown.com

Blog:
christenbrown.com/blog

Facebook:
/christenjbrown

Pinterest:
/christenjbrown

Also by Christen

CREATIVE SPARK

ONLINE LEARNING

Embroidery courses to become an expert embroiderer.

From their studio to yours, Creative Spark instructors are teaching you how to create and become a master of your craft. So not only do you get a look inside their creative space, you also get to be a part of engaging courses that would typically be a one or multi-day workshop from the comfort of your home.

Creative Spark is not your one-size-fits-all online learning experience. We welcome you to be who you are, share, create, and belong.

Scan for a gift from u